250
Tips, Techniques
and Trade Secrets
for Potters

D.

250
Tips, Techniques and Trade Secrets for Potters

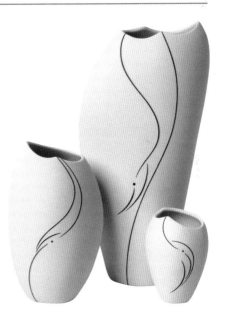

Jacqui Atkin

A QUARTO BOOK

First published 2009
A&C Black Publishers Limited
36 Soho Square
London W1D 3QY
www.acblack.com

ISBN: 978-1408-110-188

QUAR.TTSP

Conceived, designed, and produced by
Quarto Publishing plc
The Old Brewery
6 Blundell Street
London N7 9BH

Editor: **Liz Dalby**
Art director: **Caroline Guest**
Designer: **Paul Griffin**
Picture researcher: **Sarah Bell**
Photographer: **Geoff Morgan**
Illustrator: **John Woodcock**
Creative director: **Moira Clinch**
Publisher: **Paul Carslake**

Colour separation by **Modern Age
Repro House Ltd., Hong Kong**
Printed by **1010 Printing
International Ltd., China**

9 8 7 6 5 4 3 2 1

Contents

1 MATERIALS, TOOLS AND EQUIPMENT

2 DESIGN

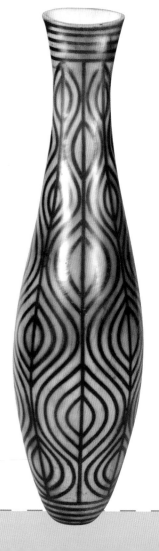

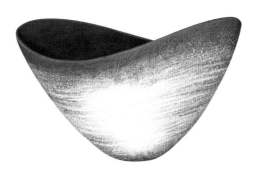

Foreword

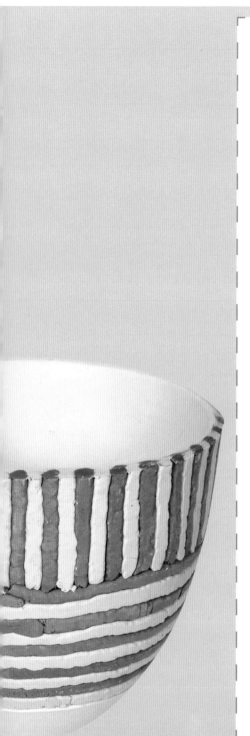

When I was learning pottery I would often struggle with a process or technique because I thought there were very set rules for working with clay; then someone would come along and show me a simpler way of working that revolutionized my understanding of a technique. Often, it was the simplest of tips that helped, and with time I realized that we all develop our own ways of working and that while there are some standard practices that are essential to learn, even these are open to interpretation.

This book will guide you through inspirational and informative techniques (including details that are often taken for granted) that will dramatically simplify your working practice, allowing you to concentrate on the more creative elements of working with clay. Here is a wealth of basic technical knowledge, with handy timesaving tips presented in easy-to-follow articles to ensure a professional finish to all your ceramic projects. Each chapter is arranged in a logical sequence to include building and altering basic shapes to create new forms and suggestions for correcting mistakes. You are encouraged to explore the fantastic range of clays, tools and equipment available with suggestions for how to choose them, and how to make useful tools from everyday objects to save money and meet your own specific needs.

All topics are fully explained and illustrated by step-by-step photography and detailed artworks for ease of use. Even the mysteries of the design process are unravelled by giving simple starting points for inspiration and development – with an index of outline shapes so that you can always create uniquely exciting ceramics.

Whether you are a beginner or a more advanced maker there is always something more to learn, so browse through the pages to find a new approach to a technique or refer to the comprehensive index for specific topics and break a few rules of your own.

Happy potting.

About this book

Insider secrets
The text is packed with tips and knowledge to help you save time and money and still get fantastic results.

Comparisons
A range of options are discussed where there are choices, for example in clays (as here) or glazes.

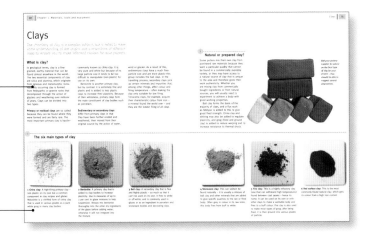

Artists' examples
Many of the techniques are illustrated with inspirational examples, demonstrating what is possible to achieve.

Techniques
All the main techniques are covered in detail, from the basics through to developing your creativity.

Instructions
Techniques are explained in detail, with easy-to-follow step-by-step instructions.

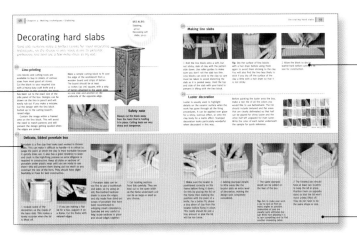

Photographs
Step-by-step photographs clearly demonstrate the key techniques.

Inspirational ideas
The directory (pages 148–153) contains an array of shape and form ideas for different kinds of decorative wares. Copy or adapt them to your own designs and preferred methods of making.

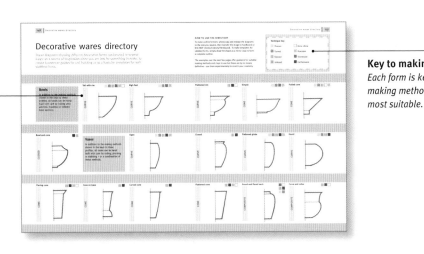

Key to making methods
Each form is keyed to the making methods that are most suitable.

Chapter 1

Materials, tools and equipment

Find out about the properties of a range of clays to suit
your needs; discover tips for storing, handling and
preparing clay; and get the low-down on the essential
tools to get you started – from major investments such
as kilns and wheels to smaller modelling implements.
There are also plenty of ideas for tools you can
improvise from everyday household objects.

Clays

The chemistry of clay is a complex subject, but it helps to have some understanding of the origins and composition of different clays to enable you to make informed choices for your projects.

What is clay?

In geological terms, clay is a fine-grained, earthy material that can be found almost anywhere in the world. The two essential components of clay are silica and alumina, which originate from igneous and metamorphic rocks. Naturally occurring clay is formed from feldspathic or granite rocks that decomposed through the action of glaciers and weathering over millions of years. Clays can be divided into two types:

Primary or residual clays are so called because they can be found where they were formed and are fairly rare. The most important primary clay is kaolin–

commonly known as china clay. It is very pure and white but because of its large particle size it tends to be too difficult to manipulate (non-plastic) for use on its own.

Bentonite is another primary clay, but by contrast it is extremely fine and plastic and is added to less plastic clays to increase their plasticity. Because of their whiteness, primary clays form the main constituent of clay bodies such as porcelain.

Sedimentary or secondary clays differ from primary clays in that they have been further eroded and weathered, then moved from their

original source by the action of water, wind or glacier. As a result of this, sedimentary clays have a much finer particle size and are more plastic–this group includes the ball clays. In the travelling process, secondary clays pick up certain minerals and impurities that, among other things, affect colour and firing temperature – often making the clay only suitable for low firing. Terracotta clays, for example, acquire their characteristic colour from iron – a mineral found the world over – and they are the lowest firing of all clays.

1

The six main types of clay

1 China clay: A high-firing primary clay – non-plastic on its own but a common component in clay recipes and glazes. Molochite is a vitrified form of china clay that is used in various grades as a pure white grog in many clay bodies.

2 Bentonite: A primary clay that is added to clay bodies to increase plasticity. Use in measures of up to 2 per cent in glaze mixtures to help suspension. Always mix bentonite thoroughly into the other dry ingredients of the glaze before adding water; otherwise it will not integrate into the mixture.

3 Ball clay: A secondary clay that is fine and highly plastic – so much so that it can't be used on its own. It fires to white or off-white, and is commonly used in glazes or as an ingredient in porcelain and stoneware bodies and decorating slips.

Natural or prepared clay?

Some potters mix their own clay from purchased raw materials because they want a particular quality that cannot be found in a commercially available variety, or they may have access to a natural source of clay that is unique to the area and therefore gives their work authenticity. Whether you are mixing clay from commercially bought ingredients or from natural sources, you will usually need to experiment to achieve a body with good working properties.

Ball clay forms the basis of the majority of clays, and a flux such as feldspar is added to this to give good fired strength. China clay and whiting may also be added to regulate plasticity, and grog (fired and ground clay) is added to reduce warping and to increase resistance to thermal shock.

Ask your pottery supplier for advice on the best type of clay for your project – they should be able to suggest several alternatives.

4 Stoneware clay: This can seldom be found naturally – it is usually a mixture of ball clay and other minerals that are added to give specific qualities to the raw or fired body. Often grey in colour in its raw state, this body fires from buff to white.

5 Fire clay: This is a highly refractory clay (one that can withstand high temperatures) found between coal seams – hence its name. It can be used on its own or with other clays to make a workable body and fires to a buff colour. Fire clay is also used to make most types of grog; after being fired, it is then ground into various grades of particle.

6 Red surface clay: This is the most commonly found natural clay, which gets its colour from a high iron content.

3 Processing natural clay

This process is similar to reclaiming clay (see page 18). If you are mixing clay from powdered raw materials: weigh out the ingredients, mix them together in a bucket then cover with water and process in the same way.

1 After digging up your clay, let it dry out completely before attempting to process it – then break it down by crushing with a rolling pin, hammer or mallet.

2 Place the clay in a bucket, cover it with water, and allow the mixture to break down into a suspension of solid in liquid.

3 Strain the clay slurry through a mesh to remove stones and other organic material, then allow the slip to settle in a bucket over several days.

4 Siphon all excess water off the clay – a large sponge is perfect for this job – then pour the clay slip onto a plaster bat. The slip will dry very quickly, so turn it regularly to stop it hardening too quickly.

5 Peel the clay off the plaster bat, then wedge and knead it to a workable consistency – it will benefit from being rested for a while before testing, so seal it in a plastic bag while you wait.

4 Clay recipes

Clay bodies are readily available from suppliers in powder form so that you can mix your own, but here are a few recipes to try if you want to make your own clay from basic ingredients.

Basic stoneware:
Fire clay 60%
Ball clay 20%
Feldspar 10%
Silica 10%

Low-temperature stoneware:
Fire clay 50%
Ball clay 20%
Frit 25%
Silica 5%

Basic porcelain:
China clay 25%
Ball clay 25%
Feldspar 25%
Silica 25%

White-firing stoneware:
Fire clay 30%
Ball clay 20%
China clay 20%
Frit 25%
Silica 5%

5 Buying and storing clay

The amount of clay you need to buy will be dictated by your output and the way you work. Throwers generally get through clay much quicker than hand builders because the process is faster. When hand building, a few bags of clay will last quite a long time, especially if you reclaim all your scraps. However, one of the main factors dictating how much clay you buy will be storage space.

Tips
- Keep clay in tightly sealed bags to retain moisture; preferably in a dark, cool, but frost-free place. Old fridges make great storage containers for clay because they do not rust and are airtight – remove the shelves to maximize the space.
- Check the clay from time to time to make sure it is not drying out. If it appears to be getting too hard try wrapping it in an old wet towel and sealing it back in the bag for a few days – this will usually return it to a workable condition. You could also try piercing the bag the clay is in with a series of holes then stand it in a bucket of water for a few hours. Drain the clay and seal in another plastic bag until you are ready to use it.
- If all else fails, simply chop the clay into smaller pieces, allow it to dry completely, then reclaim it. Clay never needs to be wasted.

Clays vary greatly in colour, texture and firing range.

TRY IT

7 **Testing your clay**

You will need to test your clay to ascertain four key properties:

Plasticity: Test the plasticity of the clay by rolling a small coil then bending it into a curve. If it splits and breaks it is too short and will need the addition of a more plastic clay such as bentonite or ball clay – try adding up to 30 percent by degrees until you have the right consistency.

If the clay is too sticky it will need the addition of non-plastic clay to give it "tooth". This can be introduced in the form of grog, which should be mixed into the clay in small amounts until it becomes workable.

Shrinkage: Clay shrinks in three stages – as it dries, in biscuit firing (where shrinkage is greatest) and in firing to its top temperature. On average, clays shrink between 10 and 15 per cent between their raw state and their mature fired state, depending on type. As a general rule, the higher a clay is fired, the greater it will shrink.

Porosity: The porosity of clay directly influences the amount of glaze that is absorbed when decorating and how well the glaze will adhere to the body. Firing samples to biscuit temperature should be enough to measure porosity adequately. A very simple test for porosity is to dab the surface of the clay with water – if it sinks in very quickly, the surface is obviously very porous and will take up a lot of glaze. If the water remains on the surface, the clay has vitrified and will not absorb anything.

Firing temperature: Some ingredients in clays, such as iron oxide in terracotta, act as a flux that reduces the melting temperature of the body; if fired too high it can literally melt. Other clays can be fired to very high temperatures – up to 1400°C (2552°F) before maturing. When testing your clay, fire it on scrap pieces of kiln shelf in case it melts. This way you will avoid damage to other work or good kiln furniture. If you have access to a test kiln, fire the clay in stages above 1000°C (1832°F) until you find its optimum temperature. Test the clay with and without glaze for thorough analysis.

6

Measuring shrinkage

Roll samples of your clay into 15-cm (6-inch) long strips, then scratch a 10-cm (4-inch) line down the centre of each one. Measure the scored lines at each of the stages of firing to assess the percentage of shrinkage. It may help to make up to three samples so that you can compare them all together afterwards.

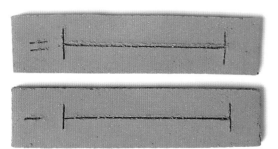

SEE ALSO:
Preparing clay,
18
Firing clay,
20

Ready-made clays

Pottery suppliers now have a huge selection of ready-made clays to meet almost all needs. They will be able to advise you on your specific requirements if you tell them what you want to make, how you want to fire it, and what function it will have.

8

Deciphering information in the clay catalogue

Clays are usually classified into three main types – earthenware, stoneware and porcelain – which are differentiated by their fired density and the strength of the ware. Within these classifications there are many variables. To make your choice, you really only need to ask yourself three questions. Once you have answered them you will have a good idea of the type of clay you will want to use. The samples on the following pages will give you some ideas for choosing the right type of clay for your project if you are still confused.

What temperature do I want to fire to? This will determine whether your clay should be earthenware or stoneware. Both types can be used for all making methods but earthenware will need to be glazed to make it waterproof, so bear this in mind if you want to make domestic ware. Stoneware will fire to biscuit without glaze. Extreme firing processes such as Raku will require clay with good thermal shock properties that has been grogged.

Does the colour of the clay matter? If you want your clay to form a contrast to surface decoration (as in slip-resist techniques for example) then colour is very important. White clay forms the best base for many coloured glazes, though for the Majolica technique you would choose red clay. Some clays are specifically made to react with glazes – to form speckles or other surface features – but could spoil your work, if this is not a deliberate choice. Generally the supply catalogue will state this feature of the clay, so be sure to read all the information before making your choice.

What making technique do I intend to use? It is no use choosing a heavily grogged body if you want to throw because it will cut your hands to pieces, so choose a smooth or finely grogged clay instead. Grogged bodies are generally more suitable for hand building – available in grades ranging from fine to extremely coarse; the catalogue will list the making methods that are best suited to specific clays.

Samples of earthenware bodies

Texture scale: 1 = smooth, 10 = coarse

Grogged red earthenware, half-covered in clear glaze
Choose this clay for sculptural and garden ware. The clay fires to a light red colour, becoming darker the higher it is fired. Because of the addition of grog, this clay will fire higher than standard earthenware. At the lower end of the firing range the clay must be glazed to make it waterproof – the body only vitrifies at the top of the firing range.

Firing range: 1040°C–1240°C
(1904°F–2264°F)
Texture scale: 8

Standard red earthenware, half tin-glazed
The glaze breaks over textured areas and the clay develops a "toasted" appearance around the edges of the glaze, becoming darker towards the top of its firing range. This type of clay is suitable for all making methods – especially thrown ware – and is used for Majolica decoration (tin glaze with painted oxide decoration). The body must be glazed to make it waterproof.

Firing range: 1060°C–1160°C
(1940°F–2120°F)
Texture scale: 5

Low temperature white body, half transparent-glazed
White earthenware bodies are made primarily from a mixture of ball clays and other minerals and are generally chosen as a light ground for colour decoration. This type of clay is most suitable as a throwing, machine-making or casting body and needs to be glazed to make it waterproof.

Firing range: 1060°C–1160°C
(1940°F–2120°F)
Texture scale: 1

Samples of stoneware bodies

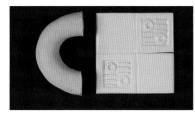

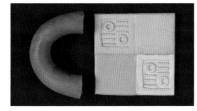

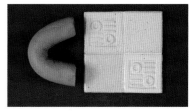

Smooth white stoneware, half transparent-glazed
This fires to an off-white colour. It is suitable for throwing – even large pieces – but is also suitable for modelling and hand building where a smooth body is required. It forms a good base for coloured glazes.

Firing range: 1220°C–1280°C (2228°F–2336°F)
Texture scale: 5

Buff stoneware, one quarter transparent-glazed, one quarter tin-glazed
This is a dual-purpose clay with a fine texture which, when fired to earthenware temperatures, is a yellow/buff colour, but is dark gray with slight speckling when fired to stoneware temperatures. It is an all-purpose clay and is suitable for both hand building and throwing. It is relatively inexpensive so is a good choice for beginners.

Firing range: 1120°C–1280°C (2048°F–2336°F)
Texture scale: 5

Heavily grogged stoneware, one quarter transparent-glazed, one quarter tin-glazed
The addition of sand or grog increases strength and resistance to warping. Use this type of clay for slab work and large-scale hand building – the clay fires to a speckled buff/grey colour. It can also be used for Raku firing where a more open, grogged body is required to cope with thermal shock.

Firing range: 1200°C–1280°C (2192°F–2336°F); also low Raku temperatures of up to 1000°C (1832°F)
Texture scale: 9

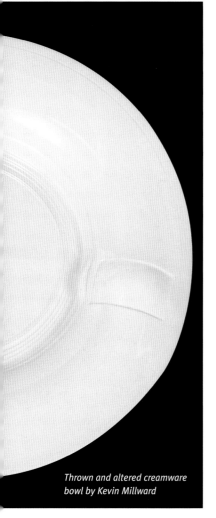

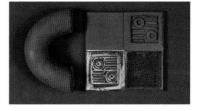

T material, half transparent-glazed
This body is made from a blend of low-shrinkage clays and calcined china clay (molochite) and has excellent plasticity, low shrinkage and a wide firing range. It is the perfect clay for extreme firing processes because it has an amazing tolerance to thermal shock and is suitable for all hand building methods of any scale. It is relatively expensive, so try mixing it half-and-half with a less expensive one that fires to the same temperature. Many potters mix it with porcelain.

Firing range: 1200°C–1280°C (2192°F–2336°F); also an excellent body for extreme, low-firing techniques such as smoke firing or Raku
Texture scale: 8

Black stoneware, one quarter transparent-glazed, one quarter tin-glazed
Black-firing stoneware clays have great potential where colour contrast is required. This clay has very low shrinkage, is strong and warp-resistant and is available in three grades of texture – smooth, medium and coarse. This sample is suitable for any hand building method but is especially good for tiles, relief panels and murals. The smooth version is suitable for throwing and hand building, while the very coarse variety is good for rugged sculptural forms and architectural ceramics.

Firing range: Medium and smooth 1080°C–1260°C (1976°F–2300°F); coarse 1160°C–1260°C (2120°F–2300°F)
Texture scale: 8 (this sample); smoother version 7; coarse version 10

Thrown and altered creamware bowl by Kevin Millward

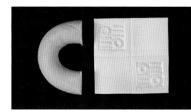

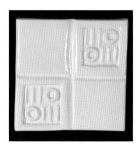

Standard porcelain, half transparent-glazed

Porcelain has a fine particle size and is the least plastic body to throw or hand build with. There is a narrow margin between being too soft and too dry when working with this clay, which makes timing critical. But it has wonderfully translucent qualities at high temperatures, which make it the perfect body for certain types of ware and it is the perfect base for transparent glazes that develop wonderful density of colour, especially when they pool in surface marks.

Firing range: 1220°C–1280°C
(2228°F–2336°F)
Texture scale: 1

Special white porcelain, half transparent-glazed

This type of porcelain is now widely available although it is much more costly than the standard variety. You can see quite clearly how much whiter it fires and for this reason is the choice of potters who use resists to create different layers in the clay to show translucency. Use in the same way as standard porcelain to throw or hand build.

Firing range: 1220°C–1280°C
(2228°F–2336°F)
Texture scale: 1

Bone china made from casting slip, half transparent-glazed

Bone china used to be the whitest firing body of all until recent developments in white clays. It is the most difficult clay to work with and takes considerable understanding to fire properly without warping or cracking. It is most suitable for casting and machine making techniques and is not a good choice for a beginner. Unusually this clay is fired to its maturing temperature at the biscuit stage with subsequent glaze and decorative firings at lower temperatures. However, this clay can be cast beautifully thinly, is white and translucent and has supreme fired strength, so for many potters there is nothing to compare with it.

Firing range: 1240°C (2264°F) biscuit,
with glaze firing from
1080°C–1140°C
(1976°F–2084°F)
Texture scale: 1

It is a measure of the skill of the maker that this clay could be thrown at all because it is so coarse, but as these samples by Kevin Millward show, it is possible if you have a spare 30 years to practise your technique.

This smoother example shows the contrast between the two versions of the clay.

Samples of paper clay bodies

Paper clay has the ability to stick to itself whether wet or dry, thick or thin – it is a truly amazing material! It is quite possible to make slabbed vessels from bone-dry paper clay sheets. Just cut the slabs to the required dimensions then assemble the parts by first dipping the edges in more paper slip – it acts as glue and is an instant fix. In the same way you can build onto a form that may be bone-dry – when coiling, pinching or modelling – simply re-wet the edges and continue to build.

Paper clay can really be used for all making methods but without the limitations that many clays impose by their nature and composition.

Ready-made types are also available.

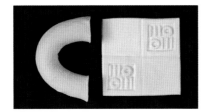

Porcelain paper clay, half transparent-glazed

This clay has all the qualities of porcelain but with the inclusion of paper is a much more workable material – even for beginners. Use for all hand building techniques.

Firing range: 1220°C–1280°C
(2228°F–2336°F)
Texture scale: 2

Grogged paper clay, one quarter transparent-glazed, one quarter tin-glazed

The addition of grog to this paper clay makes it particularly suitable for large scale and sculptural work – model-making, tiles and other hand building techniques.

Firing range: 1100°C–1280°C
(2012°F–2336°F)
Texture scale: 6

TRY IT

9 Making your own paper clay

1 Mix powdered clay into slip with water. The slip should resemble thick cream when thoroughly mixed. Wear a mask to avoid inhaling rising dust as you mix the slip.

2 You can buy paper fibre from your pottery supplier; it can be quite dusty, so wear a mask when mixing it. Put the paper fibre into a bowl or bucket and cover with water. Allow it to saturate completely.

3 Squeeze the water from the paper pulp then mix it into the slip thoroughly. You can use the mixing blade for this. Because of the water content in the pulp the slip will get runnier as the two ingredients are mixed together – this is normal, but if it looks too runny, simply add more paper pulp.

4 Pour the paper clay onto a plaster bat and smooth over the surface to spread it evenly. Turn it regularly to keep it from drying out too much on the underside. When it is a workable consistency knead it into a block and store it in plastic until you are ready to use it. In this form you can use it to soft slab, pinch, coil or even throw.

Tip
Try using a metal mixing blade attached to an electric drill to thoroughly blend dry ingredients into water. Any number of heavy-duty mixing jobs can be done in the same way in the pottery studio and this can often save the need to sift things.

SEE ALSO:

Agate,
60–63

Preparing clay

How you prepare and treat your clay is perhaps the single most important consideration for a successful outcome.

10

Pain-free reclaiming

All spare scraps of clay can be reclaimed for further use, although this can be a tedious process which most potters avoid doing until they really have to. There are some tips and techniques that make the job easier and quicker.

1 Allow your clay scraps to dry out, then break them into small pieces and place them in a large plastic container. Completely cover the clay with water and allow it to soak overnight – this process is called "slaking down".

2 Siphon off the excess water from the bucket. Give the clay slurry a little mix then transfer it to a plaster bat to form a thick layer.

3 Turn the clay over on the bat from time to time to make sure it dries evenly then, when it is a workable consistency, remove it carefully. You will find it will roll off the bat quite easily. The clay is now ready to wedge.

Tips
• Recycle your clay regularly, in smallish amounts to avoid the job becoming a mammoth chore.
• If you use hot water rather than cold, your clay will slake down much faster.
• A wheelbarrow is very useful for reclaiming larger amounts of clay. Drill a few holes in the base of the barrow and line it with heavy-duty fabric – old jeans are good – then fill the barrow with slurry. The barrow can be wheeled outside into the sun – the excess water will drain away and the clay can be left outside until it is dry enough for wedging.

11

A technique for wedging

Wedging mixes the clay thoroughly and removes air bubbles that could otherwise cause explosions during the firing process. The technique shown can be used to blend two or more clay types together or to combine hard and soft clay for a better working body.

1 Stack up sheets of the clays to be combined in alternate layers then beat the pile into a brick shape with your hand.

2 Holding the block of clay in one hand, allow one end to drop onto the work surface so the other end is raised slightly. Position your cutting wire under the raised end at the centre of the block and cut through.

3 Lift one half of the block, and throw it forcibly on top of the other half. Beat the clay back to a brick shape then repeat the process until the clays are completely combined.

Two kneading methods

Water is constantly evaporating from clay – kneading helps to redistribute it and makes the clay easier to work with. You should always knead your clay before beginning to work.

Tip
Knead only enough clay to complete your project and keep it wrapped in plastic until you need it.

Spiral kneading

1 Place your hands on opposite sides of a roughly rounded lump of clay. Push down on the clay with your right hand while rolling it forward, using your left hand to contain the clay and prevent sideways movement. Rotate the clay with the left hand after each movement.

2 A cut through the clay mass from time to time will show a developing spiral as the clay evens out. Continue to rotate the clay anticlockwise, moving the right hand into position for each downward push. Try to develop a rhythm when kneading in this way.

Ox-head kneading

1 Position your hands at opposite sides of the top of the clay mass with your fingers wrapped around the sides. Push the clay down and away from you. As you push down you will see a raised mass remaining in the centre. Roll the clay back towards you then reposition your hands slightly forward and repeat the process.

2 Continue to rock and push the clay until it is smooth and thoroughly mixed, with no air pockets.

TRY IT

Adding textures to clay

Many potters add other materials to their clay to produce special effects or textures. The most common ingredient to add is clay itself, in the form of grog. This improves the strength of the clay and helps to reduce warping.

Dry porcelain crushed into chunks gives a heavy texture to the clay and produces softened lumps when fired.

Feldspar kneaded into stoneware clay will produce beautiful soft eruptions in the surface.

Grit and aggregate give a good, heavy texture for making sculpture. Some particles will melt while others remain as rough-edged chunks.

Grog is fired and ground clay that is added to a clay body to increase strength and texture.

Coarse molochite is available in very large particles for coarse sculpture work.

Fine molochite is a good substitute for grog where retaining the whiteness of the clay is essential.

• Grog made from red clay often breaks through the clay body to create spots in the surface glaze – speckling stoneware glazes especially if reduction fired.
• White clay bodies are grogged with molochite (calcined china clay) because it does not alter the colour at all.
• Feldspars and granite chips can be added to clay. These ingredients melt at very high temperatures to produce interesting eruptions on the surface but aggregates and other refractory materials can also be added – they will not melt but they do fuse into the clay and can be ground down later to form smooth, rocklike surfaces.

SEE ALSO:
Larger equipment,
28–31

Firing clay

Clays are usually fired in two stages – the first stage is known as "biscuit" firing and it is at this stage that the clay shape is made permanent by an irreversible chemical process (although it remains porous). The purpose of biscuit firing is to make the pots easy to handle for glaze application. The second stage, known as the "gloss" firing, melts a glaze onto the surface of the clay and this can be achieved using a range of atmospheres and techniques such as Raku, oxidation and reduction.

Basic biscuit firing technique

Biscuit firing should be started slowly, so that the temperature rises at 100°C–150°C (210°F–300°F) per hour until it reaches 500°C (930°F). At this temperature, the water in the clay molecules is driven off so the rate of temperature rise can be increased. Most potters biscuit fire from 960°C–1000°C (1760°F–1830°F).

Gloss firing

"Oxidation" is the term used to describe the process of firing a glaze in the presence of oxygen, and usually this happens in electric kilns. Most beginners will fire their work in this way as it is the simplest method. The adequate supply of oxygen during firing will ensure that any oxides present in glazes will remain intact – therefore oxidation colour responses will result. For example, copper oxide will produce greens.

"Reduction" firings usually take place in wood-, gas- or oil-fired kilns; the reduction atmosphere is caused by the burning of carbonaceous material. The reduction phase of a firing usually starts at somewhere between 1000°C and 1060°C (1832°F and 1940°F) and involves cutting off the supply of oxygen to the kiln as the temperature increases to about 1280°C (2336°F). As the carbon

in the burning materials exceeds the oxygen present in the firing chamber, incomplete burning occurs, and carbon and carbon monoxide form. These then take oxygen from the oxides present in the clay and glazes to create a "reduced" effect that directly influences the colours obtained from oxides; copper oxide, for example, will produce red.

Tip
The process of reduction firing can be quite technical, so look for courses or workshops that will allow you to experience the reduction firing process before investing in the necessary equipment for the technique.

Tips
- Make sure your work is completely dry before firing.
- Stack pots on top of or inside other pots to maximize your kiln space – it does not matter if pots touch for biscuit firing. Make sure stacked items are equally weighted – heavy pots sitting on lighter-weight pots would cause problems.
- Don't wedge the bases of pots inside the rims of others – the clay needs space to shrink or it will crack.

- Leave the bungs out of the kiln until 500°C (930°F) has been reached and the water driven off. You can test this by holding a glass over the bung hole for a second or two – if it steams up, there is still water, so wait until the temperature has risen another 50 degrees or so and then try again. Don't hold your hand too close to the hole because you could burn yourself – wear protective gloves if possible.

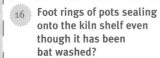

FIX IT

16 **Foot rings of pots sealing onto the kiln shelf even though it has been bat washed?**

Try firing the pots on a thin layer of silica sand spread carefully over the kiln shelf. The particles of sand act like tiny ball bearings, allowing the clay to move easily as it shrinks and reaches its top temperature. Be careful not to spread the sand too close to the edges of the kiln shelf because it could fall onto the work on the shelf below and will ruin the surface of the glazes.

17 **Pots warping and cracking excessively?**

This could be caused by several things:
• Uneven thickness in the walls of the pot will cause distortions as the clay shrinks – it does not particularly matter if the clay wall is thick or thin as long as it is even.
• Clay memory – uneven distortion of clay in the making process will cause distortions as the clay shrinks in firing, especially at high temperatures. This is because clay particles align in a specific way in the making process and the clay will always revert to the shape it was first formed into once fired.
• Very plastic clay will tend to warp more – try adding sand or grog to even out the body.

Firing high temperature clays: stoneware and porcelain

Gloss or glaze firing: 100°C (212°F) per hour up to 450°C (842°F), then kiln on "full" up to a top temperature of 1200°C–1300°C (2192°F–2372°F).

Tips
• All pots should have clean bases and feet with all traces of glaze removed, otherwise they will stick to the kiln shelf.
• Don't support stoneware pots on stilts – place them directly on the kiln shelf to give adequate support. The clay may bend and slump at high temperatures if it is not on a firm base, and will sink over stilts.
• Pots must not touch each other or the kiln walls when glaze firing because they will stick together. Space them apart so that you can just pass your hand sideways between each item – this will allow enough space so that any glaze bubbling or dripping will not affect surrounding items.

Firing low temperature clays: earthenware

Biscuit firing: 100°C (212°F) per hour up to 500°C (932°F), then 150°C (302°F) per hour up to 1150°C (2102°F). A higher biscuit temperature is used with low-firing clays to reduce crazing in the glaze. The clay remains sufficiently porous for glazing at this temperature. There may be some variations in the maturing temperature of some low-fire clays but your clay supplier will be able to advise you on this.

Gloss or glaze firing: Most earthenware glazes fire to between 1060°C and 1080°C (1940°F and 1976F°). Start the glaze firing slowly – 100°C (212°F) per hour – up to 450°C (842°F), then accelerate the rate up to the required temperature (kiln on "full").

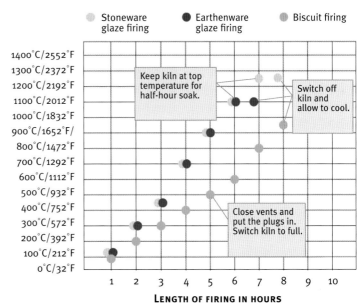

This kiln chart shows the approximate cycles for firing your pottery. The numbers show how many degrees per hour the temperature should rise for successful biscuit, earthenware and stoneware firings. You may find you need to make small adjustments to these figures to suit your own kiln.

SEE ALSO:

Setting up your
workspace,
86–87

Basic tools

There are some basic tools that you will need to buy, but in
many cases these can be replaced with cheaper alternatives.
Here and in the next few pages are a few essential basics,
along with some ideas for alternatives where possible. More
specific tools are described in some of the technique sections.

Scraping and cutting tools

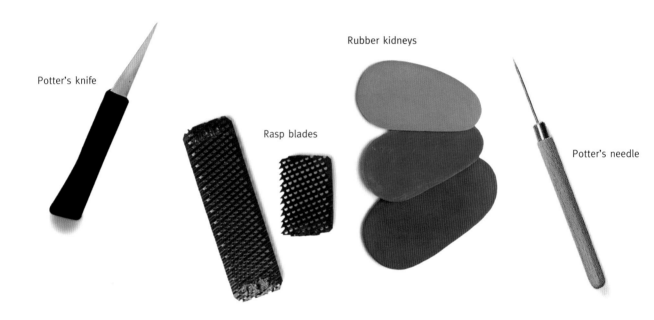

Potter's knife

Rasp blades

Rubber kidneys

Potter's needle

20 Potter's knife

*You will often need a knife when
potting, and the potter's knife is
a good shape for many needs,
but craft knives (available in
cheap multipacks) also work very
well. Alternatively, a hacksaw
blade sharpened at one end will
do the job, and the serrated edge
makes an extra tool.*

21 Rasp blades

*A rasp blade is an invaluable tool
that is used to pare down clay
surfaces, level rims and create
decorative surface textures. The
blades are available in several
sizes, but try using old cheese
graters – the various sizes can
make really great textures.*

22 Rubber kidneys

*It is advisable to have at least
one rubber kidney along with
those made of other materials,
because often your work will
require a very flexible kidney to
smooth and compact its surface.*

23 Potter's needle

*A potter's needle is useful for
marking levels on rims prior to
cutting, piercing holes or
releasing air, but a simple
alternative is a hat pin pushed
through the end of a bottle cork
or glued into the end of a
discarded ballpoint pen. The pen
top can then be used to cover
the pin when not in use.*

Ribbon or
loop tools

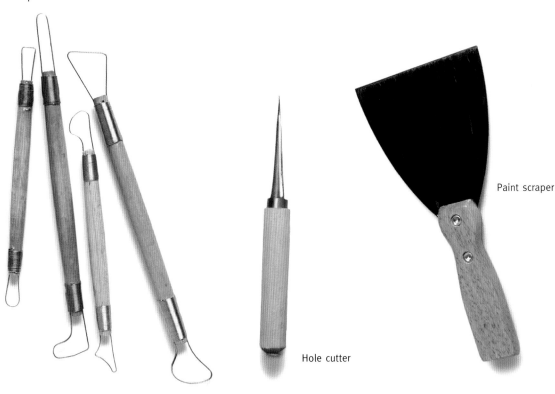

Paint scraper

Hole cutter

24

Ribbon or loop tools

Ribbon or loop tools are used mainly to trim the bases of thrown pots, but also to hollow out handmade shapes, especially sculptural forms. Alternatives can be adapted from many things including some kitchen implements. Many potters make turning tools from the metal banding used to seal packing boxes, which is strong and yet flexible enough to be shaped to your requirements.

25

Hole cutter

Hole cutters are available in different sizes, usually with a tapering metal blade that is rotated as it is pushed through the clay. Make your own from plastic pipes – available in many sizes – simply cut a chamfer at one end of a 15-cm (6-inch) piece of pipe with a wood saw or hacksaw. The cut can then be easily smoothed off with sandpaper. Or try a refillable ballpoint pen – when unscrewed, the pen can be inserted and rotated into the clay to make the hole. The plug will be contained inside the pen and can be removed with a pin. The small end of the pen makes great buttonholes.

26

Paint scraper

A paint scraper is a useful tool for cleaning the wedging bench, work surfaces and boards – you can probably find many alternatives in your kitchen drawers, including metal spatulas, carving knives and so on.

Forming tools

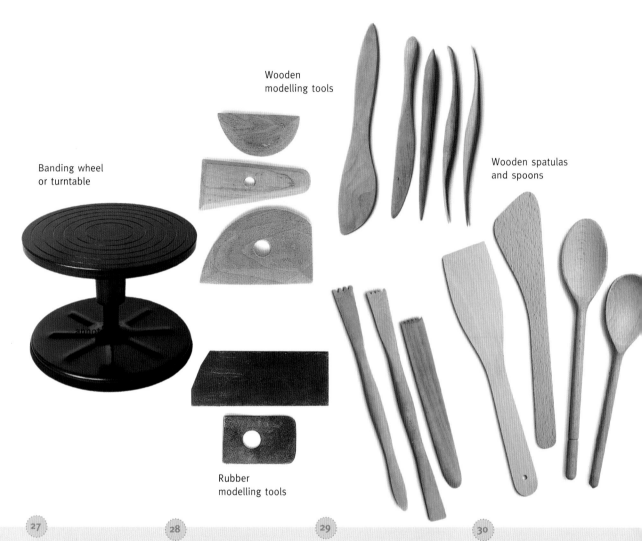

Wooden
modelling tools

Banding wheel
or turntable

Wooden spatulas
and spoons

Rubber
modelling tools

27 Banding wheel or turntable

A banding wheel or turntable is not strictly essential but will make most tasks easier, because the work can be viewed from all sides. A lazy Susan makes a really useful alternative if you can find one.

28 Roller guides

Roller guides are available from most DIY stores in varying thicknesses. It is much cheaper to buy lengths and cut your own than to buy these from a pottery supplier, but remember that you will need two of each.

29 Wooden or rubber modelling tools

These are probably best bought from your pottery supplier but you should only need two or three to serve most functions – don't be tempted to buy more than you need.

30 Wooden spatulas and spoons

Easily sourced from the kitchen, wooden spatulas and spoons are highly versatile for beating, smoothing and texturing clay. (Do not reuse them in the kitchen afterwards.)

Decorating tools

Calipers

Slip trailers

Brushes

Sponges

31
Calipers

Calipers are used for measuring the widths of lids and galleries in the throwing process and are inexpensive to buy from your pottery supplier.

32
Brushes

Good brushes are essential and should include soft, moplike varieties, like the hake, for applying slips and glazes, and small paintbrushes for applying under-glazes and lustre. Old toothbrushes are useful for scoring and slipping the clay surface and can be used as spattering tools for slip or glaze. Shaving brushes are good for brushing away bits of clay when carving or incising.

33
Sponges

Sponges are essential for removing excess water from the insides and surfaces of pots. They can also be used to apply slip and glaze decoration. You should have a selection of both natural and synthetic sponges with one fitted to the end of a stick for reaching into tall and narrow forms when throwing on the wheel.

34
Slip trailers

Slip trailers have a range of uses and are available in different sizes, but also look for plastic cosmetic bottles with fine nozzles (many hair products come in nozzled bottles) – they make excellent alternatives.

SEE ALSO:
Ideas to make things easier, 87

Improvising tools

Every trade needs tools and pottery is no exception, but commercially bought tools can be very expensive and are often inadequate for precise making needs. Many everyday items can make useful tools, but you can also make them to your own specific needs from materials that would otherwise be thrown away – so not only do you save money, but you get to do your bit for recycling in the process!

Onion holder

Comb

Saw blade

Rolling pin

Garlic press

Cutting wires

Saw blade

35 Texturing tools

Use onion holders, old combs and saw blades for scoring edges and creating simple surface texture finishes.

An old garlic press makes a superb extruder for clay – great for making hair when modelling or for creating other textures.

36 Rolling pins

Rolling pins are often not long enough to roll large slabs. Try making them from old curtain poles or the wooden poles that are used for roller blinds. These can easily be cut to the required length.

Try cutting and drilling patterns into old rolling pins that are no longer good enough for rolling smooth slabs. These can be fantastic for making textured slabs. Even the simplest marks will make great repeat patterns.

String or yarn wrapped randomly around a rolling pin also works well.

37 Cutting wires

Cutting wires break easily. Make your own from fishing line, which is available in various strengths and comes in rolls that will last for years, at just a fraction of the cost of commercial wires.

Curtain rings or duffle coat toggles make really good handles. Make a selection of different lengths to meet different needs.

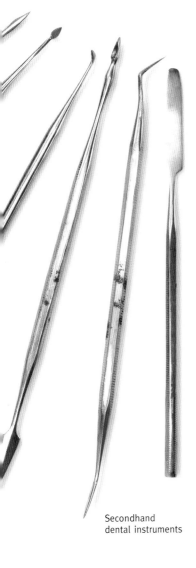

Secondhand dental instruments

Plastic scraping tools

Try some of these:

1 Basic kidney with different-sized notches cut out for finishing the rims of plates and dishes.
2 Long scraper with different shaped angles for reaching into difficult areas – for scraping and smoothing, this also makes a good burnishing tool.
3 A toothed end is good for scoring edges and texturing patterns.
4 Specifically shaped tool for curved areas.
5 Pointed end – useful for chamfering the bases of thrown pots while still on the wheel.
6 Shaped for finishing off rims and foot rings.
7 Smaller kidney for awkward shapes.
8 Basic kidney shape for scraping and smoothing.

TRY IT

40 Making your own scrapers

Use these templates to make your own shapers and scrapers from plastic – old credit cards are perfect!

Modelling tools

Garage sales and charity shops are great places to find alternative tools such as old dental instruments. Costing hardly anything, they make fantastic modelling tools. Most are double-ended and there is a different shape to meet every possible modelling need.

Scraping tools

Use old credit cards or plastic spatulas to make your own kidneys and scrapers. These are fantastic tools because they can be made quickly and easily to meet the needs of the specific pot you are working on. Some templates are shown in the panel, above right.

TRY IT

41 Creating textures with DIY equipment

You can use almost anything to add an interesting texture to your work. Try impressing fabric, wallpaper, craft stamps or even leaves – anything bumpy, in fact! Always test new objects on an offcut of clay first to check that they will not adhere to the surface.

38 39

SEE ALSO:
Firing clay,
20–21

Larger equipment

There are some larger pieces of equipment that are essential for a pottery studio – the kiln being the most important – and of course a wheel for those who want to throw. These items will be the most expensive things you will have to buy. The following tips should help you make your choices.

42

Buying a wheel

The pottery wheel is a very expensive piece of equipment so you should perfect your hand building skills initially to assess your interest and dedication before you invest in one. Wheels are available in a variety of sizes – try a few out before purchasing one to find which suits you best. Look out for secondhand wheels – the internet is a good place to start looking, but pottery suppliers often have reconditioned ones for sale and many are advertised in the classified section of ceramics magazines.

Wheels are available in three types: kick wheel (below right), momentum and electric (above right). The type you choose should be based on the amount of work you intend to produce and the ease of working. Generally, electric wheels are the easiest to use for speed of production and for making large pots. They are available in a variety of sizes, some have integrated seats, and others can be adjusted in height and more easily moved, with remote foot pedals.

wheel head. Both the momentum and kick wheel are difficult pieces of equipment to learn to throw on because they require the extra coordination of the foot along with the hand-eye coordination of the throwing process.

- Kick wheels are propelled by a pedal or crankshaft that is operated by the potter's foot spinning a flywheel.
- Momentum wheels work in a similar way in that they are operated by the potter. They have a large, heavy flywheel that is powered by the feet or a stick placed in a notch on the

43

Kilns – which type?

Kilns are available in a range of sizes, from small mains-operated hobby kilns to massive commercial ones that require a special power supply to run. Gas kilns can be obtained if you wish to make reduction stoneware – again in several sizes – smaller ones are also useful for Raku firing. Wood firing kilns are generally built in situ, in rural areas, because of the fumes they put out. So, before you make a choice, here are some points to consider:
- Electric kilns are the best choice for the beginner – they burn cleanly and come in a range of small sizes.
- Sophisticated programmers mean that you do not have to "kiln-sit".
- Top-loading kilns (left) are usually less expensive than front loaders – they are also easy to install.

- Front-loading kilns (opposite page) usually have a very solid metal framework with a more substantial firebrick wall, but are consequently heavier and retain heat for much longer. They are more expensive to buy and install but much harder-wearing than a top-loader.
- Gas kilns need to be housed in an outside building with ample space and ventilation. They fire from natural or propane gas and give off fumes that will need venting.
- The reduction firing process is more complicated than oxidized firings, requiring the maker to kiln-sit in order to program the different stages of the firing. Programmers are available at great cost but are mostly for very large kilns in commercial use.

New vs old

If you can afford it, buy a new kiln because older kilns tend to be heavier, less efficient, more expensive to fire, and may need overhauling. However, great bargains can be had from people who bought new kilns then lost interest in pottery. Search the internet for such bargains.

If you decide to buy new, most pottery suppliers will have a good range of kilns to choose from and will be able to advise you on the best size and type to meet your needs. It pays to shop around – often a supplier will do you a deal if you say you have found something cheaper elsewhere.

 Kiln furniture

Kilns are packed using shelves and supports. Tubular props are available in different sizes and are stackable to allow you to adjust the height of the shelves. Triangular star stilts are used to raise earthenware glazed work off the kiln shelf. The points at the ends of the legs break off after firing, leaving small marks that should be ground down.

KILN SAFETY

• The kiln should not be sited in the room where you work. If there is no other option, you should fire it overnight so that you are not in the room during firing.
• Site the kiln away from flammable materials or structures, and leave enough space to move around it easily.

• Make sure the floor of your workshop can support the weight of the kiln and can tolerate heat.
• VERY IMPORTANT – a top-loading kiln can be hazardous for people who suffer with back problems – especially when lifting large or heavy work up, then over and down into the firing chamber. A front-loader is a safer choice.

• Gas kilns are available in updraught and downdraught systems that further complicates choice, although the downdraught version is generally considered to be more efficient. There are also two types of burner to choose from – the naturally aspirating type (used for Raku) or the economical, package or forced-air burner that is more efficient and easier to control.
• Wood firing kilns are mostly the choice of diehard potters who are happy to feed the kiln through many hours – even days. Such kilns are generally only fired a couple of times a year and therefore need a lot of work to fill them, a lot of wood to fire them, a rural environment to fire them in and great patience and stamina. Great fun for some!

FIX IT

 Confused? Ask yourself these questions:

What space do I have to house a kiln?
This will to a large extent dictate the size of the kiln.

What is the accessibility to the kiln site like?
A large kiln will not fit through a little door. Also consider how you will move a heavy kiln from the delivery vehicle to site.

What power supply do I have?
An electric kiln will need an electricity supply – and large kilns often need a bigger supply than most domestic situations provide. If you choose gas you will need space to house your propane bottles as well as the kiln unless you use natural gas, which will have to be piped to site.

What scale of work do I want to make and how much at a time?
If you need to fire something in a hurry and your kiln is big you will waste precious energy. It is far better and more economical to fire a small kiln more often.

Raku kilns

Raku kilns can be bought from ceramic suppliers in several sizes or built from firebricks or high-temperature insulating bricks. Alternately, they can be made from metal drums or wire-mesh cages lined with ceramic fibre for insulation. Commercial gas burners are widely available and make firing quick, clean and easy. Your ceramic supplier should be able to advise you on the best type for your kiln if you provide specifications. Most Raku kilns are fired using propane gas.

- Before you begin, the work to be Raku fired should be made from an open, grogged body that has good thermal shock resistance, and should be biscuit fired.
- Once glazed, your pots must be dry before you pack them into the Raku kiln, so apply glaze the day before so that they can dry out overnight.

- Don't pack too many pots into the kiln at once – two or three is more than enough to handle in one firing – many potters only fire one pot at a time, especially with larger pieces.
- Support the pots on triangular star stilts so that they are raised off the kiln floor.
- Be meticulous in your preparation for firing – have everything you need at hand for a smooth operation. Your smoke bin should have a layer of wood shavings in the bottom and another container with more shavings close by. The bin lid should be within easy reach to clamp down quickly when required. Tongs should be within easy reach and you should have somewhere safe to place the hot kiln lid when you lift it off.
- Make sure the smoke bin is close to the kiln so that you don't have to lift the hot pots far. The bin can be moved away after the pots have been put into it.
- Position the kiln on a good flat surface.
- Fire with a friend – for safety and the sheer fun and enjoyment of the experience – it is good to share!

Raku firing
The firing procedure usually takes place outside because of the fumes which are generated. Rapidly fire the pots until the glaze melts, somewhere between 800°C and 1000°C (1472°F and 1832°F) – this should take approximately 20 to 30 minutes. The glaze should look smooth and liquid with no bubbles on the surface.

Lifting the pots out
Wearing heavy-duty gloves and a respirator, lift the lid off the kiln and put it somewhere safely to one side then lift the pots out of the kiln with metal tongs.

Tips for experimental firings
- Pack the pots in layers of different grades of sawdust – from fine to shavings – for interesting markings.
- Wrap the pots in other materials like straw, seaweed, banana skins, leaves or horsehair before packing.
- Try soaking strips of fabric in brine – then wrap the cloth around the pots and fire them. Secure the cloth with copper wire for added effects.

FIX IT

 49 **Worried about the environment?**

- Both Raku and smoke firing can make a lot of noxious smoke, which can be unpleasant and dangerous to inhale directly but will have little impact on the environment otherwise.
- If firing in an urban environment, make sure you will not upset your neighbours by firing your kiln. Be considerate – don't fire if they have washing on a line, for instance, and ask if they have any concerns beforehand so that you can explain what you are doing. Try not to fire so often that you are always producing smoke – it can become very annoying.

50

Using a smoke bin

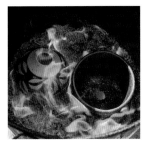 

1 Transfer the glowing pots to the bin of wood shavings. Be careful – it will ignite quickly. Cover the pots with a little more of the shavings then seal the lid. Because of the rapid cooling process, pots undergo intense thermal shock, which causes the glaze to craze, allowing smoke to penetrate through to the clay body. This gives the familiar crackle effect.

2 Many pots can be left in the smoke bin until they cool down – others will need to be removed to a secondary chamber (without shavings) to cool down if you want the effects of the smoke to be more subtle. Be careful – wear gloves and a respirator to handle the work, and be aware that the wood shavings can easily reignite once the lid is removed.

51

TRY IT

Improvising a kiln for smoke firing

Smoke firing is a low-firing technique, so the pots should not be biscuit fired above 1000°C (1832°F) otherwise they will not be porous enough to absorb the carbon from the fire. Smoking is best combined with burnishing, and the surfaces can either be left undecorated to simply show the marks of the smoke, or patterned with masking tape and clay resists for very dramatic effects.

Metal bins of all sizes can be used for smoke firing: this is the simplest and least expensive option. You can smoke fire in sawdust, straw or newspaper and it will help if you drill a few holes around the sides of the bin to help with the passage of air.

Cleaning the pots
Use a scouring pad and a cream cleaner to remove carbon marks from the surface of glazed pots when they are cool enough to handle.

52

Smoking in newspaper

Pots covered in paper and clay resists are best smoked in newspaper. You will need to repeat the process several times for good results. Place the pot in a bin filled with loosely scrunched newspaper then set it alight and allow it to burn down.

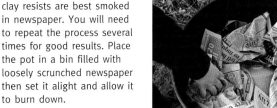

Tips
• Cover the bin with fine-mesh chicken wire to keep ignited bits of paper from flying out.
• Pots without resists can be packed in sawdust and simply allowed to burn down slowly.

Tip
Never plunge your pots into cold water to cool them down – having gone to the time and trouble of carefully making your pots, why risk them exploding simply to speed up the cooling process?

Chapter 2

Design

All designers sometimes need a starting point. In this chapter you can find ideas for kick-starting the creative process. Get hints on where to look for your initial inspiration and then see where your research takes you. And before you get started making, experiment with sketches, card models or even mini versions.

Developing ideas

All makers sometimes struggle for new ideas to rejuvenate their work. But if you have been through a training process, design will have been part of the course and you will be equipped with skills to help you resolve things. For those who have not had any formal training, the idea of design is often quite scary – but the techniques and tips on the following pages will help to ensure that you are never short of ideas. Try them out – you'll be surprised how easy they are, and you should never be lost for inspiration again!

TRY IT

53 Finding inspiration

Collect objects: Try taking a shopping bag with you when you are out for a walk in the country or along a beach. Pick up anything that interests you, and you will find you rarely come home without something to inspire you – it could be anything with an interesting shape, texture or colour. You can also buy such things from more exotic places to add to your collection if you wish. Try internet auction sites for ideas.

Research: Look at the work of other potters – this is always a good place to begin to understand what type of ceramics you are drawn to and may want to try making yourself. You will find that your preferences will broaden as your understanding of the processes and your abilities grow.

Visit museums and galleries: Look at historical examples of pottery. You will be amazed by the skill and complexity of some ancient works and there is much to learn from them.

Visit libraries: A library is always a good place to research your particular interests, but the internet is now also a fantastic information resource. Look at the websites of particular potters – or general sites such as the Craft Potters Association.

Gather visual information: Look at and cut out pictures from old magazines and catalogues, postcards, flyers, leaflets and so on.

54 Where do I start?

Start off on the design route simply by looking at things. Everything will have some potential for inspiration if you know what to look for. If something attracts your attention, ask yourself why. Is it the shape or the colour? Maybe it has a surface quality or pattern that particularly appeals, or it could be simply be the way that light interacts with it. Get into the habit of recording visual information with photographs or sketches.

Photographs
Carry a camera with you everywhere to capture photographic reference – point-and-shoot digital cameras can be small enough to carry in a pocket and are relatively inexpensive. Alternatively, many mobile phones include a camera.

Sketches
Try making quick sketches in a pocket-sized book of the things you see. A sketchbook is like a diary – it is for your eyes only. It does not matter if you think you can't draw because nobody else need see it. However, most people can record an approximation of the things they see and, providing you record the essential elements of what has inspired you, that is all that matters. Annotate your sketches as an aide-memoir, and glue images that you like alongside them.

Making sense of your research material

Once you have collected plenty of information, you can proceed in several different ways.

Resource file

Make a resource file of interesting images. Considerations should include colour – this example shows images in a mainly warm colour range, including reds, oranges and yellows. Colour-theme the file, starting from black and white and working through the colour spectrum.

Form: include images that suggest possible shapes for your pots.

Texture and pattern: look for images that you think could be reproduced or interpreted in clay in textural form, or that suggest surface decoration.

Mood board

A good alternative to the resource file is to make mood boards of interesting images. This will allow you to work on a larger scale and include more information, but the considerations for content are essentially the same. Include colour swatches from paint companies (available at most DIY stores) – these will help you to decide on a possible colour palette for your work.

Viewing frames

Cut out a selection of viewing frames in different shapes and sizes from stiff card. This will allow you to view areas of the enlarged image in isolation from the rest to extract more information. Look for interesting combinations of line and form, then either draw the details directly into your sketchbook or trace them.

Working from images

Work directly from photographs or other images – enlarge them on a photocopier so that you can see details more clearly.

Tracings

Trace areas of interest from the enlarged image and transfer them to your sketchbook. If it helps, reproduce the image in as many ways as you can think of, add shadow or colour, isolate areas even further and pick out details that you like – this is often easier to do when working with a traced image.

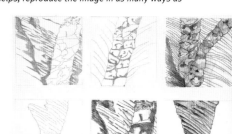

Developing form

By this stage you should have enough information to suggest ideas for the shape of your body of work.

Isolate your image

Isolate your chosen image and draw it lightly on a separate page of your sketchbook, then start to develop the shape – make subtle changes to the form and dimension and add new features. If your drawings, or even the original image, suggest how you might want the surface of the work to look, incorporate these ideas into your drawings or make notes.

Brainstorm

Draw out any developments that occur to you or make notes to remind yourself later – you may want to incorporate a feature that was not suggested by the original image. This is good – allow your mind free rein to come up with ideas.

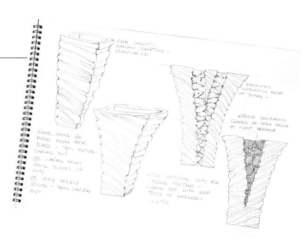

Maquettes

If you have the time you can make either two- or three-dimensional maquettes of your form. Score and bend card outlines of your forms to spark ideas for surface finishes.

Clay samples

Make clay samples to explore possible surface treatments that will have to be made at the building stage of the form. Experiment with different tools to create texture, or combine clays for colour variations. Consider combining clays that fire at different temperatures for interesting effects – be bold and explore as many possibilities as are feasible.

Mini versions

Build miniature, three-dimensional versions of your form to help resolve the practicalities of making it to actual size. This is your chance to get the visual weight and balance right. If there are unforeseen problems with the work, it is much easier to iron them out at this stage, before making the real thing.

57

Making methods

At this stage of the design process you will probably have decided on the best making method for your form. If it is very large the chances are you will need to coil or slab-build it; smaller items could use the same techniques or be pinched or thrown. You may want to make a plaster mould to slip-cast the form, or it may be that you need to experiment further to find another method. The one you thought you would use may not be practical, but by following

basic design principles you should be able to resolve problems before actually making the work.

Most of the basic techniques for surface decoration are included in this book and don't require design making, but there might be occasions when you will need to work out a pattern in advance of applying it to the surface of your work, especially if it needs to form a repeat. The following tips will ensure you get it right first time.

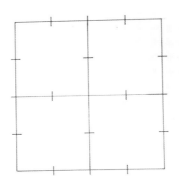

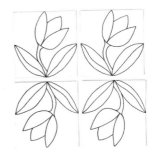

Simple symmetrical repeats

Patterns like these are especially good for tiles or slabbed vessels. Draw a box and divide it into four. The size of the box should relate to the size of your work – in this example, each quarter of the box is the size of the tile that the pattern is going to be applied to. Mark as many equal distant points on the sides of each box as you require for your pattern.

Draw and trace the design

Draw your design into one of the boxes making sure it touches the edges at the markers. Trace the design, then repeat as desired; the pattern should repeat when rotated, flipped or mirrored.

Tip
Keep it simple – even though there are only four points marked in this example, they are enough to allow for the pattern to repeat well. If you add more markers, things get more complicated and take more working out.

FIX IT

58 **Patterns not lining up?**

Before applying the pattern to your work, ensure that each repeat lines up properly with the markers by cutting the square into four and rotating the quarters in all directions.

Chapter 3

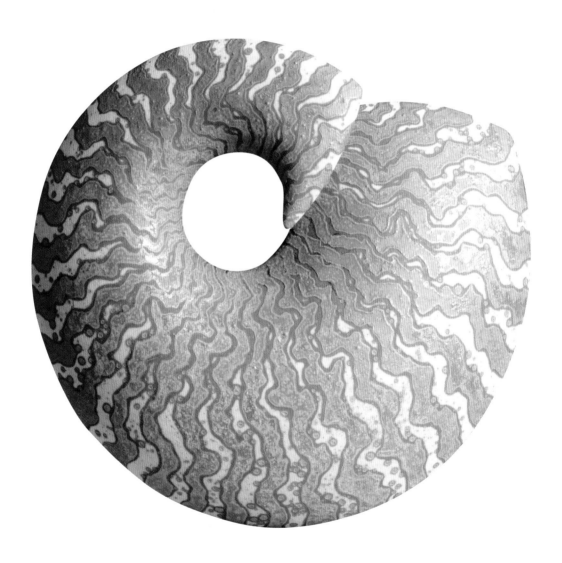

Making techniques

This chapter deals in-depth with the main techniques: slabbing, pinching, coiling, throwing and mould-making, as well as glazes and various firing methods. It's packed with insider tips to help you get the most out of any technique. Common problems are solved and there are lots of ideas for extending the basic principles for a world of exciting experimentation.

SEE ALSO:
Ready-made clays,
14–17
Preparing clay,
18–19

SLABBING

Slabbing is the term used to describe the technique of making clay objects from sheets of clay. It is a versatile and exciting way of working that allows great scope for experimentation for making anything from domestic ware to sculptural pieces. Slabs can be made in several ways and the method of making is a personal choice. It is also determined by the type of object you intend to make and the clay you want to make it from.

TRY IT

60 A cheap alternative to a harp

A harp is a relatively expensive piece of equipment. Try this as a good alternative for cutting slabs:
• Cut a length of batten into equal-sized strips. Stack the strips up in two piles of equal height on either side of a lump of clay.
• Hold a cutting wire taut and draw it along the uppermost strips of wood to slice off a slab. Remove a strip of batten from each stack. Cut the next slab in the same way.

You can make slabs from any clay using this method (even very thin ones) because the thickness is determined by the depth of the wooden strips.

It helps to have a selection of wooden batten strips of different thicknesses to allow you to cut thicker or thinner slabs according to the type of clay or project you intend to work on. Batten is readily available in various sizes from most DIY stores.

59 Cutting regular slabs

A clay harp is a good way of cutting smaller slabs of regular size and thickness. The mechanism works by adjusting the wire down a notch each time a slab is cut. Use firm pressure to keep both sides of the harp rigid and firmly on the work surface because the wire will otherwise rise as it cuts through the clay making the slab very uneven. Draw the wire through the clay from front to back.

This method is particularly suitable for tile making where a lot of slabs need to be made quickly. Form the lump of clay into the correct size for your tiles prior to cutting, which will save having to cut them to size again later.

61 Making larger slabs

You can make larger slabs by joining smaller ones together: simply overlap the edges of the slabs, then blend the two surfaces together using your finger or thumb. Turn the slab over and repeat the blending process on the underside. Smooth over the slab with a scraper to even out the thickness when all the sections have been joined together.

All clays except porcelain (which is generally prepared in much thinner slabs) are suitable for this method of making. Unfortunately the notches on harps are generally too widely spaced to make really thin slabs.

62 Reducing thickness

To reduce the size of a large lump of clay to a manageable thickness prior to rolling, beat the clay evenly across its surface with the side of a rolling pin. Turn the clay over and through 90 degrees and then beat it again. Continue to do this until the lump is adequately flattened. Try using the side of your fist as an alternative if you can't get the hang of using the rolling pin – the key to success is to keep the clay as even as possible as you reduce it in size – try to avoid deep impressions from the rolling pin or your hand because these can cause weaknesses in the slab.

63

Making thin, even slabs

1 This is a method that requires a little practice but once mastered is a great way of making thin, even slabs quickly. Cut a piece of clay from a lump then, holding it in both hands so that it hangs down, throw it onto the work surface.

2 Lift the slab from another edge and turn it around so that when you throw it onto the surface again it lands on the other side. Repeat the throwing process until you are satisfied with the thickness of the slab.

Because this method is generally used to make larger slabs the most suitable clay to use would be a grogged variety that is robust during handling.

Rolling

To make slabs of even thickness place two wooden roller guides on either side of your lump of clay before rolling out with a rolling pin. Each end of the pin should eventually rest on the guides as the slab thins out.

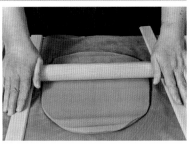

FIX IT

64 Problems with large slabs?

If a large slab seems unevenly thick when all the smaller slabs have been joined together, use the heel of your hand to push the clay out again where it is thickest – then smooth over the surface with a rolling pin or scraper to finish.

If you are making large slabs it is generally advisable to use grogged clay for extra body and strength. You can buy this type of clay ready-made from your pottery supplier who will advise you on the best type, or simply wedge 8 to 10 per cent grog or sand into your clay, which will greatly increase its wet strength (its ability to keep its shape during construction).

FIX IT

65 Slab ripping?

• The clay is probably too wet to begin with – try wedging it on an absorbent surface to remove some of the excess water, then throw it again.
• Be careful to hold the clay flat between your fingers and thumbs without bending them – digging fingers into the clay causes it to tear easily.
• Don't let the slab hang too long in your hands before throwing it – the whole process should be completed in a few seconds.
• If the clay does tear, simply overlap the torn edges, blend them together, then rethrow the slab – it is never irreparable.

66

Making rolling easy

It is almost impossible to roll out large slabs of clay in one go, so you will need to turn the clay. To make this easier, roll the slab on a sheet of plastic. Start to roll the clay from the middle of the lump, first rolling forward, then back – this will avoid a mass of clay developing at the centre.

1 Roll the clay in one direction until it becomes difficult to roll any further, then lift the slab on the sheet in one hand, turn it over onto the other hand, peel off the plastic, and replace it on the work surface.

2 Turn the slab through 90 degrees and replace it on the sheet of plastic, then roll again, making sure the roller guides are in place either side of the slab.

Repeat this lifting and turning process as often as necessary until the rolling pin rolls easily over the guides.

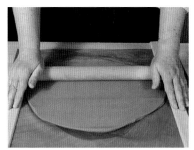

SEE ALSO:
Slabbing,
40–41

Forming slabs

Slabs can be formed into shapes in two ways: when the clay is in a soft state that allows the shape to be manipulated as it is built, or when it has firmed up sufficiently to hold its shape without support.

Soft or hard slabs?

Soft slabs are used to make softer, organic-type forms; therefore the slab is usually shaped while it is still pliable. Soft slabs can be wrapped around formers to make vases or other vessels, over or in plaster and other types of mould, or in purpose-built slings. They can be made into sculptural forms, or even domestic ware – the possibilities are endless.

Hard slabs are allowed to dry to the leather-hard stage before being used to construct more angular, sharp-edged forms such as boxes or larger sculptural pieces.

Key factors for successful slabs

- The most important thing to be aware of when building with either soft or hard slabs is that the stresses on the joins should not be underestimated – if edges are not securely joined they will open up or crack in the firing process.
- The thickness of the clay must be even throughout the construction – it does not matter how thick or thin the slabs are, as long as all sections are the same. Inconsistencies will cause uneven drying, which in turn will cause warping and cracking.

Maquettes

Design and construct your forms in thin card before you commit to clay. These models are called "maquettes", and will give you the opportunity to see how the form will work and allow you to make any necessary changes. You can then dismantle the maquette and use the sections as templates to cut the required shapes from the clay.

Slab-built female figure by Christine Keeny, coloured with stains and oxides.

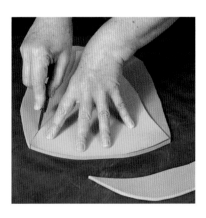

Mitring the edges

If you are planning to make slender, two-sided forms from your slabs that will need a fine join, it helps to mitre the edges of the shape before you form it. If you are working with hard slabs, you can use a ruler to steady the knife as you cut the mitre; however this cannot be done with a rounded shape, so practise on scraps of clay to get the technique right before you begin. Cut the mitre, holding your knife at a 45-degree angle with the point touching the work surface at all times. Work from one corner to the middle of the section only to begin with. Now turn the shape around and cut from the opposite end to the point where the first cut ended. This will avoid damaging the edges as you get to the end of the cut.

Tips for perfect joins

The traditional method of joining edges is by scoring them with a knife or other sharp tool then applying slip, but this can be time-consuming. By using an old toothbrush and water in the same way that you would to brush your teeth, you can achieve the same effect – the brush scores the edge as you work it and the water naturally turns the clay to slip in the process.

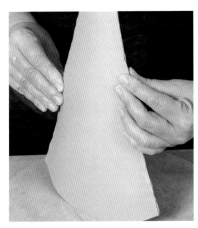

Pinch edges together gently but firmly between fingers and thumbs, making sure the sections are aligned correctly.

Using a small printing roller is a great way of neatening edges and has the added advantage of further securing the seal.

If the edges distorted at all during construction, simply use a metal kidney to remove any excess clay and refine the shape back to the original outline.

TRY IT

Using a sling mould to form rounded slabs

Make a simple sling mould from wooden battening and fabric. Cut and assemble the frame to your required size. Use metal corner angles to fix the sections together, then turn the frame over and pin a sheet of heavy-duty cotton or similar fabric to the wood so that it dips gently towards the middle to form the sling. Make two frames if you want to form more than one section at a time.

The sling will naturally form the slab into a more rounded shape but you can develop it more using a rubber kidney and your fingers. You can then allow the slab to dry to leather-hard naturally, or use a hair dryer to speed the process along a little. A hair dryer is probably the most useful tool a potter can use because it reduces the time it takes for clay to dry to a workable state.

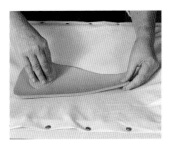

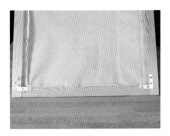

72

Reinforcing joins

Always reinforce joins on slabbed forms unless they are totally inaccessible. Use thin coils of soft clay and work them along the seam, blending the clay in, using your finger or a wooden tool. Take care with this, because you must avoid trapping air between the seam and the coil, which could force the seam apart in the drying or firing process.

Sponge or foam is great for supporting work in construction, especially if the form has an irregular shape. Look out for bubbly varieties as shown here – it is often used in packaging and is particularly useful.

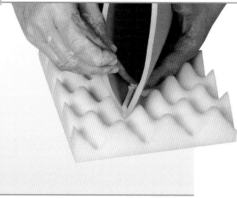

Butt-edge joins

Some seams are easier to put together by butting one edge up to another instead of by mitring. This technique is more suitable if you are not sure how well a section may fit, because it gives scope for making adjustments after the sections have been joined.

73

Cutting sections for butt-edge joining

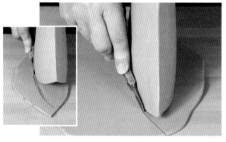

1 One of the simplest ways of making sure your base sections are going to fit properly is to cut them exactly to the shape of the form after the first sections have been joined. Simply sit the form onto a pre-prepared slab of clay, then cut around the base.

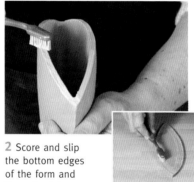

2 Score and slip the bottom edges of the form and the cut-out base section really well before joining them together carefully.

3 If your form has a rounded base, as in this example, you can roll it from side to side on the work surface a couple of times to help secure the base to the body. If the form is flat-bottomed, simply tap it gently on the surface a few times.

4 Paddle the underside edges with a wooden spatula to secure the join completely. Wooden spatulas like these are readily available in lots of shapes and sizes from most kitchen shops and are much cheaper to buy than those purpose-made for pottery.

5 Use a blade to carefully shave away excess clay along edges. Blades like these are available in curved or flat form in several sizes from most DIY shops. They are great tools for this purpose but can also be used to level rims, reduce the bulk of weighty pots or texture the surface of clay.

6 Use metal scrapers and kidneys to finely smooth and blend joined edges together and refine the shape of the form.

74

How to support slabbed structures

1 You can use thick or thin wooden dowel to support structures – such as this soft slab animal – as they are made. The dowel should be long enough to allow the form to be suspended with plenty of space for you to work on the body.

2 Added support can be given to structures such as these by simply placing a small piece of folded card between the clay and dowel prior to forming. This will prevent any further supports from breaking through the clay as the body and legs are worked on. The card will burn away when the animal is fired.

3 Limbs can be formed around smaller lengths of dowels.

4 Cotton wool helps to retain the shape during construction. It can often be removed later when the form has firmed up but will otherwise burn away during firing.

5 Use balls of clay to hold the leg supports in place as you close the front and rear of the form. Clay can be used as support in all sorts of ways and can be manipulated into any supporting shape you need.

Dowel can be used as a support and also as a former for details such as the pig's tail.

75

Useful objects to use as formers

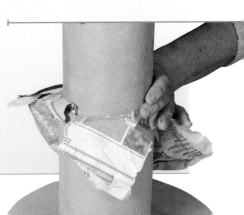

Always cover tubes with newspaper before wrapping slabs around them – this will make them much easier to remove later. If you don't do this, the clay will almost certainly stick to the tube making it impossible to remove. Slide the tube out first, leaving the newspaper in place. Don't worry if the paper does not come out – it will burn away later when the tube is fired.

Tiles
Old ridge tiles are great for forming slabs over. Ask for slightly damaged ones at a builders' suppliers – they may not be good enough for use on a roof but can usually still be used for ceramic purposes. You can often get them for free. Because the tiles are non-absorbent you should always lay a sheet of newspaper or fabric over the surface before placing your slab to keep the clay from sticking.

Cardboard tubes
Cardboard tubes make really useful formers for soft slabs. You can also use sections of drainpipe or even glass bottles as alternatives but cardboard tubes come in all sizes, so collect a range of them. Cylinders are the starting point from which all kinds of forms can be made.

76 Making a slab cylinder

1 Cut a slab of clay to fit around your chosen cylinder using a paper template measured to fit the cylinder and allow for about 2.5 cm (1 inch) of overlap.

2 Gently roll the clay around the cylinder until the ends overlap, then carefully mark the overlap with a knife or wooden tool. Take care not to cut through the clay.

3 Score and slip both edges of the overlap with a toothbrush and water, then join them together carefully.

4 Gently rolling the cylinder back and forth at the overlap will secure the join sufficiently to stand the cylinder up, then you can roll over the join with a printing roller or rolling pin to blend the two surfaces together. It is easy to distort the shape of the cylinder as you do this so roll from top to bottom rather than side to side. Refine the surface of the join by smoothing over with a metal or rubber kidney.

TRY IT

 78 Using vinyl wallpaper

To add textured surface decoration to the cylinder, try rolling in strips of blown vinyl wallpaper. Align the strips so that the bottom edge of the paper fits along the bottom edge of the slab. Don't roll in the strips too close to the ends of the slab because the texture will be obliterated by the overlap.
Leave the strips in place until the cylinder has been made – this will keep the texture from being spoiled when handling the cylinder during making.

Altering the shape

Once you have removed the texture strips and cardboard cylinder you can alter the shape to an oval form easily by gently squeezing the sides between both hands. Allow the form to dry almost to leather-hard before handling further. Make sure the clay is firm enough to hold its shape before

TRY IT

77 Alternative finishes

Leave the edge of the overlap unblended for extra decorative effect, so that the form obviously has a wraparound look.

Here, textured porcelain has been used to make dainty little cups from slabs where the overlap has been left to form part of the detail. The handles were mould-made in the same clay.

Try tearing the overlap edge instead of cutting it when you make the slab – rough edges make a really good feature on this type of form.

removing the support, but don't allow it to dry out too much because you will not be able to get the cylinder out or manipulate the shape afterwards.

Position the cylinder or oval form onto a slab of clay that is almost leather-hard like the body. Trim to the required shape then join the sections together, remembering to score and slip both surfaces beforehand. Smooth over the join carefully with a wooden tool or your finger.

More cylinder ideas

79

Joining cylinders

Try joining cylinder formers together to make interesting-shaped vessels. Tape them together loosely so they don't come apart during construction. Construction is the same as for the single version but with a few props.

Multi-tubular forms

Triangular-shaped strips of wood placed beneath the slab will give definition to the shape as you construct multi-tubular forms. Position one strip underneath the plastic sheet the slab has been rolled on before construction and press another piece into the opposite side when the edges have been joined.

Sculptural forms

Use simple cylinder forms as a starting point for sculptural or figurative work. Even the most basic, free modelling of a cylinder can give a form human character, but more detail can easily be carved into the surface once the basic shape has been achieved.

80

Adding decorative rims

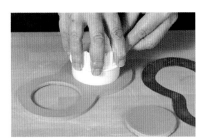

1 Measure the rim section by placing the form on a sheet of card and then drawing around the edge. Increase the outline in size by at least 13 mm (1/2 inch) all the way around. Use the template as an outline as you cut the rim.

2 Pastry cutters have many uses in the pottery workshop and are used here to cut the basic inner shape of the rim. You can either leave the rim like this, with two openings, or cut away the space between the circles to make one opening.

3 Fix the body onto the rim, making sure to score and slip the surfaces before joining. Reinforce the join with a coil of soft clay – blend the coil in with your finger or a wooden tool. Running your fingers around the rim a few times will round off the sharp edge and visually soften the profile. Don't be tempted to use a damp sponge because this has a tendency to leave the grog content of the clay on the surface, making it very rough to the touch.

FIX IT

81 **Shape collapses when the cardboard cylinder is removed?**

This means the clay is too wet to support its weight. Make sure it is firm enough to hold its shape by drying the clay off a little with a hair dryer. The clay should feel firm to the touch but still be able to be manipulated a little.

Cardboard cylinder won't come out and clay is cracking?

Clay shrinks as it dries and in this case it has usually dried out too much so that without space to shrink into it naturally cracks. Make sure the cylinder is wrapped in paper before you begin and remove it as soon as the clay can hold its weight.

Base slab separates from the body as it dries?

The most likely reason for this is that the body and base had dried to different stages before being joined together so that subsequent drying was uneven, causing stress at the join. Making all the component parts at the same time so they also dry at the same time will usually solve this problem.

SEE ALSO:

Improvising
tools, 26
Tips for decorating
at the wet
stage, 98

Decorating soft slabs

Soft slab forms are, in essence, just like any other clay surface when it comes to decorating techniques, but with some exceptions for the beginner. This section will help you to make the right choices for surface decoration with some great ideas for experimentation. If you are planning to make a form that will be tricky to put together or that will require manipulation, choose a decorating technique that is applied after construction.

A note about slip decoration

Almost all of the slip-decorating techniques (see pages 98–101) can be used on soft slab forms once they have dried to the leather-hard stage, with the exceptions of marbling and feathering. These are more suited to flatter surfaces such as tiles and dishes.

TRY IT

 Ready-made patterns

Blown vinyl wallpaper makes an excellent surface decoration if you don't want to design your own and is available in many patterns. Use the wallpaper to make a monoprinted mirror of textured decoration in your slabs.

1 Fix the wallpaper over the oxide then either rub your finger over the back of the paper to make the oxide adhere to the surface or use a printing roller, small rolling pin, or even a short length of wooden dowel to ensure a good transfer of oxide onto the paper.

2 Transfer the design to the surface of your pot with your fingers or using a roller. Clean the roller before transferring the design in case it picked up traces of oxide when making the print. Clean your hands regularly when monoprinting to avoid transferring oxide fingerprints onto the clay surface.

The transferred design

Monoprinting onto slabs

1 Paint a thick, even layer of oxide onto a non-absorbent board and allow it to dry completely.

2 Draw your design onto a piece of paper, then position the design over the oxide very carefully and secure it in place with tape. Without touching the oxide area or paper design with your fingers, carefully but firmly draw over the design again with a pointed tool or pencil.

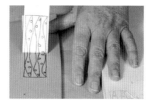

3 Carefully lift the design off the board, then position it on the surface of the clay and rub over gently with your finger to transfer the design. Lift the paper to reveal the design on the clay. Take care not to touch the monoprint before it is fired because the oxide is very easily smudged.

Use decorated slabs like these to make dishes draped over hump moulds (see page 133).

Dishes don't always have to be square! Try cutting unusual shapes for variation. This can be a good solution if your slab is too small or oddly-shaped to make a square.

TRY IT

84 Difficult but exciting!

This is a difficult technique for the beginner to master but has such exciting results that it is worth persevering to get it right. Practise on scraps of clay to begin with – you won't feel too wasteful if you don't get it right immediately.

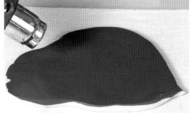

1 Paint a wash of oxide or coloured body stain over a thick slab of clay. Choose a white-firing clay for the best colour response.

2 Dry the oxide wash completely with a hair dryer. Heat guns (the kind used to strip paint) or blow lamps are great alternatives to a hair dryer for this, because they dry the surface super-fast. If you use one of these, however, you must make sure the clay is placed on a heat-retardant surface first and take great care to keep your other hand out of the way as you work. Do not touch the end of the gun after you have used it because it can cause very bad burns.

3 Score a pattern into the surface of the slab using a craft knife or similar pointed tool. Take care not to cut right through the slab.

4 The various parts of old pens are great tools for making marks in clay. Various parts have been used here to make circles of different sizes between the scored lines of the pattern.

5 Turn the slab, pattern side down, onto a plaster bat and position two roller guides on either side. Roll the slab from as many angles as possible without removing it from the bat. The idea is to distort the scored pattern on the surface beneath.

6 Carefully lift the slab off the plaster bat and place it on a board or work surface to assess the result. The slab can be cut into smaller sections and re-rolled to further distort the pattern if you are not happy with the results the first time.

FIX IT

85 Left with lots of scraps?

Don't throw the scraps away – use them to make jewellery! You can either roll the clay out thinner for fine jewellery pieces or use it as it is for chunkier necklaces and pendants. Cut circular discs using biscuit-cutters – use an old pen top to cut out a hole for the chain. Odd-shaped pieces can be cut into interesting shapes to minimize waste.

After biscuit firing

Soft slab forms can be decorated like any other form once they have been biscuit fired. Use the following ideas as a starting point for experimentation with your own work.

BEWARE

Many oxides will act as a flux when applied under a glaze, especially if thickly applied. To avoid this problem, wipe the glaze away from the base of the form and up the side by at least 6 mm (1/2 inch). This will generally allow the glaze enough room to run before reaching the kiln shelf.

TRY IT

87 Protecting your kiln shelf

The standard protection for kiln shelves is bat wash, but if you find this is not enough, try some of these tips:

• If you are worried that glaze might run off your work onto the kiln shelf, try standing it on silica sand as a precaution. Simply spread a thin covering over the shelf where the work is going to stand. The sand acts as a membrane between the work and the shelf. It will not save the work but it will save the shelf!

• A dusting of alumina can be used in the same way and is always useful when high-firing because clay can fix onto the kiln shelves even without glaze at high temperatures.

• Another good preventive measure for this problem is to make a series of biscuit-fired tiles on which you can stand your work on the kiln shelf for glaze firings. You can, if you wish, put a covering of silica sand or alumina on the tile as an added precaution. Use the scraps of clay left over when building slabs to make the tiles, so that you always have a supply ready.

86

Oxide decoration with wax resist and glaze

 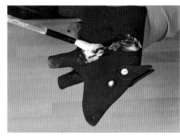

1 Paint a fairly thick oxide wash over the surface of your form, making sure it covers the whole surface (see page 70). For a more subtle effect you can gently wipe the oxide away again with a damp sponge once it has been covered. You will find the oxide will be harder to remove from around the details of the form, but this is a desirable effect that will add to the finished surface.

2 Paint over selected areas of the surface of the form with wax emulsion to make stripes, patches or marks.

3 There are several methods of applying glaze. In this example the glaze is sponged over the form using a natural sponge. Sponging a glaze lightly in this way will give a mottled effect to the finished surface. For a more even coating you should sponge the glaze on in two or three coats, allowing each layer to dry before applying the next.

When sponging glaze over an oxide surface (above), decant a small amount of glaze into a dish before you begin. Oxide will contaminate and colour a glaze very easily so it is best to only use small amounts at a time. Don't pour the glaze back into the glaze bucket once you have finished. Keep the glaze in a separate jar clearly labelled with the glaze type and the oxide you used, then you can use it again if you like the results.

Fired examples show how the glaze has reacted with the manganese dioxide wash underneath.

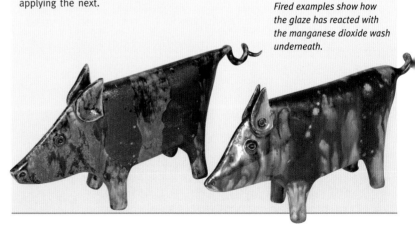

88 Glaze know-how

Whether you are using shop-bought glaze or developing your own, the principles for mixing them are the same.

1 You do not need to weigh shop-bought glaze but, if you are formulating your own, you will need a good set of scales to weigh out the individual ingredients. Bathroom scales are perfect for weighing large amounts of glaze material.

2 Put the dry glaze ingredients into a clean, dry bowl then cover them with water and allow to soak for at least 30 minutes.

3 Use a stick or wooden spoon to stir the glaze mixture as thoroughly as possible.

4 Support a sieve of suitable mesh-size on sticks suspended over a large bowl, then pour the mix in and work it through with a stiff washing-up brush or rubber rib. Sieves are available in several mesh sizes, but for most purposes an 80–100 mesh sieve is adequate. If the glaze is to be sprayed on it will need to go through a 120 mesh to ensure the particles are fine enough to pass through the nozzle of the spray.

5 The consistency of the sieved glaze should be like thick cream for most purposes. Test the consistency of glaze by dipping your finger into the mixture – it is correct if it coats your finger but allows the wrinkles to show through. If the glaze is too thick, thin it down with more water. If it is too thin, allow it to settle overnight then decant some of the water off the top.

FIX IT

89 **Glaze settled and hardened?**

Glaze has a tendency to settle and harden in the bottom of the bucket over time. You can overcome this problem by adding 1–2 per cent bentonite to the dry ingredients before adding water to mix. Do not add it after the glaze has been mixed because it will not disperse. Epsom salts can be used as an alternative to bentonite. Just mix a spoonful in water, then stir it into the mix.

90 More glazing methods

Glaze can be applied to the clay surface in several ways – by dipping, pouring, brushing, sponging or spraying. The method you choose will depend on the shape of the pot and how it can be held. You will need to consider the size of the pot and what type of effect you are trying to achieve before you begin.

Glaze can be poured over a form in several ways:
- If the form is small enough you can hold it in one hand over a container to catch the glaze as you pour. Try to pour the glaze in one even coat. This will avoid a buildup of different thicknesses. Suspend larger forms upside down on two roller guides over a container that is large enough to catch the glaze as you pour.
- Try using a funnel as a chuck.
- Invert the pot over a plastic funnel sitting inside a large bowl that in turn is placed on a whirler. This method is very good if the form has

a flared rim because it avoids glaze collecting underneath, and is possibly most appropriate for rounded forms, especially thrown vessels.

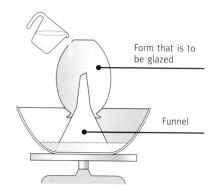

Form that is to be glazed

Funnel

91

A super-quick glaze

Dipping is a quick method of glazing for the production maker but requires a large bucket of glaze. Only choose this method if you have tested your glaze and know that you like the results sufficiently to mix up a large bucket. Simply dip the pot in and out of the glaze as quickly as possible, making sure it is completely covered. This method is possibly most appropriate for rounded forms, especially thrown vessels, but it is a useful tip to know – don't leave it in the glaze too long or it will soak up too much and be too thick. Gently shake the pot a little to make sure any surplus falls away, then clean the base with a damp sponge to remove all traces of glaze.

92

Brushing or painting

Brushing glaze onto a biscuit surface can be quite tricky because the clay quickly soaks up the liquid, making an even application difficult. Brush marks are often obvious after firing, making this the perfect technique for painterly decoration, but if this is not the effect you are trying to achieve then you would be best advised to use another method of application.

- Dipping your pots in a base glaze then brushing on another, or several, different-coloured glazes in a quick, free style can result in a wonderful abstract surface decoration. Choose glazes with good colour variations for the best effects.
- Ask your pottery supplier about paint-on glazes – there is a huge range to choose from and they are great for experimenting with, but they are expensive and come in small quantities so are unsuitable for large-batch production. If you want to glaze domestic ware, be sure to check the suitability of this type of glaze beforehand.

- Adding 2 per cent wallpaper paste to your standard glaze mix will make it much easier to brush on evenly. Choose a paste with fungicide, otherwise it will rot in the glaze mix over time.

Use a large, soft brush that will hold plenty of glaze and paint it on in short strokes, continually re-loading the brush. To avoid brushmarks being visible after firing, apply several even coats. Brushing is particularly suitable for applying Raku glazes, where differences in thickness of application can add to the visual quality of the fired work. This method is perfect for the resist Raku technique because the glaze is removed after the work has been fired.

BEWARE

- Because glaze melts to a liquid as it fires and then hardens as it cools, it will stick to any surface it comes into contact with if it runs off the pot.
- Earthenware clay generally remains porous even after firing, so all surfaces (even the undersides) will need to be glazed if it is to be used for domestic ware. To prevent the pots sticking to the kiln shelf during firing, they must be supported on three-pointed stilts, which are tapped off after firing. You will need to grind down the scars left by the stilts because they are razor-sharp to touch.

- Stoneware pots are fired to a high temperature where the clay vitrifies, making it impervious – therefore the underside does not need to be glazed. The pots are packed directly onto the kiln shelf with only a dusting of alumina or bat wash to keep them from sticking to the shelf, so they must be unglazed. Either wipe the glaze off the base after applying it, or wax the surface first to prevent the liquid glaze from adhering. It is not advisable to support work on stilts in stoneware firings because the clay can slump and distort over them as it reaches its top temperature.

TRY IT

93 Resist Raku surface decoration

The characteristic surface of resist Raku forms is crazed and dotted with black lines that are created by the radical firing process. When the fired pot is lifted out of the Raku kiln at about 454°C (850°F), thermal shock causes the glaze to contract and crack. Smoke is then adsorbed through these cracks in the reduction process. For many potters using this technique, the finish is enough to embellish the surface of their pots, but there are additional treatments that can be applied to pattern the surface further.

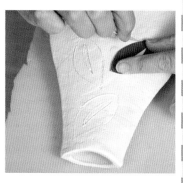

94 Slip and glaze application for resist Raku

Slip recipe: Three parts china clay to two parts flint, mixed with water to a single-cream consistency. Sieve the mixture if required.

Application: In this method of Raku firing both the slip and the glaze are used as a resist to smoke in the post-firing reduction process. This technique works best on burnished surfaces. Brush the slip over the pot making sure that no part of the surface is left uncovered. The slip can also be applied by the pouring method if preferred. Leave for 24 hours to allow the slip to dry completely.

Because both the slip and glaze are white when mixed, use food dye to colour the slip so you will be able to see if you have missed an area when glazing over the top. The dye will burn away in firing.

Glaze recipe: 45 parts high-alkali frit, to 45 parts borax frit, to 10 parts china clay. This will also work well as a transparent Raku glaze.

Application: Brush the glaze over the resist slip, again making sure that the whole area is covered. As with the slip, the glaze can be poured over the surface if preferred.

Linear designs can be scored through the glaze/slip using a pin or cherry stick. This is best done immediately after glaze application and works best if the slip and glaze layers are quite thin. You can also use outline templates to score around. Dipping the cherry slip in cooking oil before scoring the design will minimize jagged edges.

97 FIX IT

Dots but no crackle?

The pot was taken out of the kiln too soon, before the glaze had melted sufficiently for the bubbles to smooth over, therefore smoke was adsorbed through the holes, creating the black dots. There is no crackle because there is too little tension for a thermal shock reaction in the under-fired glaze.

Glaze won't come off the fired work?

The most likely cause is that the piece was over-fired so that the glaze matured and bonded with the body. The best time to take the work out of the kiln is when it resembles orange peel. Another possibility is that the glaze was applied before the slip had dried out properly. Try sprinkling the form with water to see if that helps or, as a last resort, try soaking the pot completely for two hours. If this works make sure it is thoroughly dried out again before polishing.

Specks of fired glaze on the surface of the pot?

There are several possible reasons for this:
• It could be that the slip layer did not fully cover the surface prior to glazing or was not thick enough to form a good barrier.
• The glaze could have come into contact with the surface of the pot when the pattern was scored through.
• The glaze was transferred on your fingertips as you handled the pot. This is often the case where paper resist is used.
In all cases the solution is simply to take more care when applying slip and glaze. Unfortunately, there is little that can be done to remove glaze once it has fired onto a surface.

95 Judging how to finish resist Raku

Resist Raku need only be fired to the point of a soft melt – this can easily be judged by eye. Don't over-fire the work; the glaze is there purely to form a resist for the smoke. Five minutes is more than enough time for your pots to spend in the smoke bin after firing – any longer and the patterns will blur as more smoke is adsorbed. Transfer the pot to another lidded container to cool down after smoking. When the pot is cool enough to handle, the glaze can be removed using a flexible metal kidney (although often the glaze just shells away in a most satisfying way).

Wipe away the underlying slip with a wet kitchen sponge or scourer, taking care not to rub the surface of the pot too vigorously or you will destroy the burnished surface. Allow the pot to dry out thoroughly then polish the surface with beeswax.

96 An alternative glazing method

Spraying glaze is good if the pot will be difficult to glaze in any other way. However, spraying equipment is both bulky and expensive and is therefore not really a viable option for the beginner. However, if you are lucky enough to have access to a spray booth follow these tips for success.

• Rotate the work on a whirler as you spray the glaze to ensure an even application. Spray the surface in a methodical manner, making sure runs don't develop.
• Spray the work from a distance of about 30 cm (12 in) – this will allow the glaze space to spread evenly over the surface.
• Try varying the adjustments on the spray gun to produce different effects if spraying more than one glaze onto the pot.

• Always clean out the gun after use by spraying water through it. It should then be dismantled so that individual parts can be washed to remove all traces of glaze. Failure to do this can result in cross-contamination of different glazes, which can spoil your work.
• Be careful how you handle the work after spraying because finger marks are easily transferred to the surface.

98

Decorating surfaces for smoke firing

1 Tear thin strips of clay to use as a resist over the surface of the form. Here the clay is torn to make stripes over the animal's back.

2 Fix the clay in place with some flexible wire. Often the wire will make marks as well, adding to the finished effect. Copper wire is really good for making interesting marks on clay because it melts at a relatively low temperature.

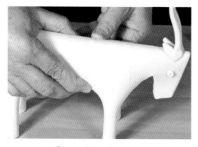

3 Another alternative is to apply torn strips of masking tape to create stripes. The tape will mostly burn away in the firing process but will resist enough to form subtle marks.

4 Aluminium foil makes a great resist material – try wrapping it around details like horns or tails to totally resist the smoke.

5 Packing different grades of sawdust around the form in the bin will give a more interesting finish. Shavings will burn faster than dust, creating different effects on the surface as they burn. Interesting marks can be achieved by packing other combustible materials around the form, instead of, or in addition to, sawdust. Try straw, seaweed, leaves or pine needles.

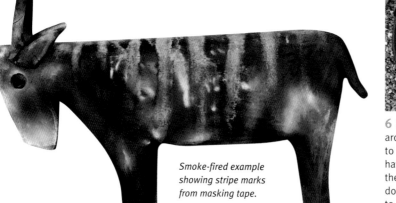

Smoke-fired example showing stripe marks from masking tape.

6 Packing scrunched-up newspaper around the edge of the bin will help to ignite the sawdust. Once you have set light to the bin and are sure the sawdust is burning well, clamp down the lid and allow the contents to burn down slowly. This can take up to 24 hours.

SEE ALSO:
Slabbing,
40–41

Constructing with hard slabs

Hard slabs are so called because they are constructed into forms when they are leather-hard. This is a much easier process than soft slabbing because the clay is self-supporting, but there are still several tips that will help to make the process successful.

100 How to make a slab box

No matter how many sections or angles a hard slab form may have, the principles for construction are the same as for this simple box – once you have mastered this, the possibilities are endless.

1 Use card templates as a guide to cut all sections of the box from a slab of leather-hard clay. Mitre both sides and the bottom edge of each of the side sections and all four sides of the base section.

Tip: When mitring leather-hard slabs, use a metal ruler placed about 6 mm (1/4 in) in from the edge to rest the knife against as you cut the angle from each end to the middle to avoid breaking the corners off.

Place a block into the angle of the joining walls to support the shape and prevent it from distorting as you join the edges together.

2 Use a toothbrush and water to score and slip all edges to be joined together. Blocks of wood make great supports for slab walls in the early stages of construction. After attaching the first side to the base section place a block either side of the slab while you prepare the next one.

3 Reinforce all the internal joins with coils of soft clay. Blend the clay into the angles with your finger or a round-ended tool. Reinforcing in this way helps to distribute stress out through the sides and away from the seams during firing.

101 Adding extra detail – feet

Attaching small balls of clay to the underside of boxes is often enough to give visual lift to a form. Position the box on four balls of clay so that a little squeezes out at the sides for best effect. Don't attach the feet until you are sure the balance is correct, then mark the position of each before joining by scoring and slipping.

You can create a different foot by cutting away the clay from the sides of the balls. Don't try to cut the balls level with the sides but simply aim to square them off.

Cut simple squares of clay to make feet in context with the shape of the box. Use a roller guide to cut a strip from a slab of clay then again to cut into squares.

Squares like these look better positioned slightly in from the edges on the underside of the box. Mark their position before scoring and slipping to join.

Simple slabbed feet

1 Cut four small sections of clay no more than 2.5 cm (1 inch) deep and the same width as the side panels then, using a biscuit-cutter, cut a small section out from one side of each section.

2 Mitre the uncut sides of the sections very carefully, then join them together as for the box (opposite). Use your roller guides to square the foot up when the sections have been joined – they help to push the corners together more easily.

3 Once the foot has been fixed to the base by scoring, slipping and reinforcing, as for the inside you can neaten up the join on the outer surface with a metal scraper, if necessary.

Adapting the technique to make other shapes

Feet and rims can be any shape you choose and you will have great fun designing your own but, if you are struggling for ideas, try out some of the shapes shown here.

Tip: Feet and rims should not look at odds with the rest of the form so, if you are not sure what details to add, cut out a few alternatives and try them out in different combinations until you are happy with the result. Unused parts can be used on another shape if well wrapped in plastic until the form is made. If you feel you are wasting clay making all these alternative shapes – make them from thick card instead. This will give the same impression as clay and you will be able to use them as templates to cut around later. It also means you will always have the template for future use.

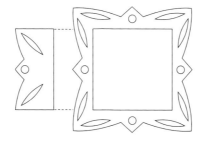

Cut-out shapes

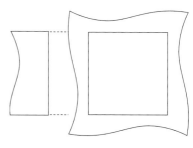

Wavy edge

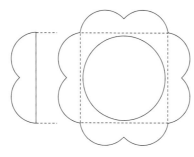

Flower shape

SEE ALSO:

Slabbing,
40–41
Decorating soft
slabs, 50–51

Decorating hard slabs

Hard slab surfaces make a perfect canvas for most decorating techniques, so the choice is very much down to personal preference, but here are a few extra ideas to try out.

106 Lino-printing

Lino blocks and cutting tools are available to buy in sheets of various sizes from most good art shops. Cut the block to your required size with a heavy-duty craft knife and a metal ruler. In this example, the block has been cut to the exact size of the side panel of the box. Designs can be drawn on the lino in pencil and will easily rub out if you make a mistake. Cut the design with the lino block butted up to the cutting board's raised edge.

Contain the image within a framed area on the lino block. This will avoid the need to match patterns and will prevent the design getting spoiled when the edges are joined.

Make a simple cutting block to fit over the edge of the workbench from a wooden board and strips of batten. The board should be at least 30 cm (12 in) square, with a strip of batten attached to the upper edge on one side and another on the underside of the opposite edge.

The finished slabbed vessel has been simply glazed to accentuate the pattern detail created by the lino block.

Safety note

Always cut the block away from the hand that is holding it in place. Cutting tools are very sharp and dangerous.

107 Delicate, lidded porcelain box

Porcelain is a fine clay that looks best worked in thinner slabs. This can make it difficult to handle – it is critical to judge the point at which the clay is most workable because it quickly dries out. It also has a great tendency to warp and crack in the high-firing process so extra diligence is required in construction. Keep all slabs or sections of porcelain under plastic wrap until you are ready to use them – this will prevent them drying out too much as you construct the rest of the form. They should have slight flexibility in them for best construction.

1 Include some of the decoration on the inside of the base slab. This makes a lovely surprise when the lid is lifted off.

2 If you are making a flat lid for a box, support it on a frame. Cut the frame with mitred edges.

3 Porcelain slabs can be too fine to use a toothbrush and water, so try using an old, fine-toothed hacksaw blade to score the edges, and slip made from dried-out scraps of porcelain that have been reconstituted to double-cream constituency. Spatulas are very useful to help locate sections in place and secure edges together.

4 Cut locating sections from lids carefully. They are best cut to the same width as the frame underneath and can be as large or small as you choose.

108

Making lino slabs

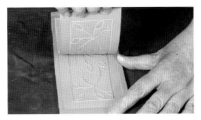

1 Roll the lino block onto a soft, but not sticky, slab of clay with the pattern side down. Use roller guides to make sure you don't roll the slab too thin. Lino blocks can stick to the clay so care must be taken to avoid distorting the slab as it is peeled away. Hold the top and side of the slab with your hand to prevent it lifting with the lino block.

Tip: Dry the surface of lino blocks with a hair dryer before using them again to avoid them sticking to the clay. You will also find the lino less likely to stick if you dry off the surface of the clay a little with a hair dryer so that it is not sticky.

2 Allow the block to dry to leather-hard before cutting it to size for construction.

109

Lustre decoration

Lustre is usually used to highlight details on the ceramic surface when the work has gone through all the firing procedures. It can be applied over glaze for a shiny, lustrous effect, or onto the clay body for a matt effect. Stamped decoration looks particularly wonderful when decorated in this way.

Before painting the lustre onto the box, make a test tile of the colours you would like to use beforehand. The tile should include textured and flat areas that are clearly delineated so that half can be glazed for shiny lustre and the other half left unglazed for matt lustre. Write the colour of each lustre underneath the sample for quick reference.

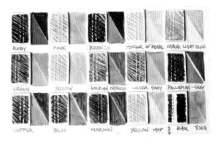

5 Make sure the locater is positioned correctly on the frame before fixing it down. Do this by placing the lid on the frame then marking the position with the point of a knife. For a better fit, shave a tiny sliver of clay from the locator before fixing in place. This really should be just a tiny amount or else the lid will be too loose.

6 Adding stamped details to little areas like the locator adds an extra level of decoration, making the design look completely considered.

7 The same stamped detail can be added on the feet of the box.

Tip: Aim to make your work a joy to look at from as many angles as possible. Undersides of pots are usually quite utilitarian but just think how pleasing it is to turn something over to find another interesting detail.

8 The finished box should have at least two locaters to keep the lid in place. Position them on opposite sides so that the lid won't move unless lifted off. They do not have to be the same shape or size.

SEE ALSO:
Ready-made clays,
14–17

Agate

"Agate" is made from the combination of two or more colours of clay to make patterns. The name is derived from agate rock, which is characterized by layers of colour.

Layering clays to make bands of colour

1 Layer two or more different clay types on top of one another and roll them together slightly. Don't roll too thin at this stage. Soft clays will bond together readily but harder clays will benefit from a brushing of slip between each layer to help adhesion.

2 Cut the layered block in half with a cutting wire then stack one half on top of the other and roll again. You can do this as many times as you like but the layers will get thinner the more they are cut and re-rolled.

3 The clay can finally be rolled to make slabs for building soft or hard forms or be used for moulding.

Staining clay

Choose white or very pale-coloured clay with the working properties you need for this type of agate. Your clay supplier will be able to advise you on the best type.

1 Place 800 g (28 oz) of dry clay that has been ground down coarsely into a bowl. Mix up some stain with a little water and pour it through a fine sieve onto the dry clay. The clay will be much easier to handle if left to stand for an hour before mixing.

Tip: You can dry clay quickly by rolling it into very thin slabs then putting it in the sun or somewhere warm. The quickest way to grind clay down for this purpose is to put it into a sturdy plastic bag then bash it with the end of your rolling pin.

2 Once the clay has slaked down, mix it into a slip then pour it out onto a plaster bat and allow it to dry until it peels off the bat easily – you can then knead it to a workable state.

Combining clays

You can layer different types as well as colours of clays together for very interesting effects. For example, mixing rough, groggy clays with porcelain will create a surface that looks like geological rock formations because of the tensions created between the different properties of the clays when fired. You can also stain the same clay different colours for a finer finish.

Tip: Coloured clays made in this way work better if made some time in advance of use. They should be wrapped in plastic and preferably stored for a couple of weeks. If you intend to make a lot of agate ware, it will help to make a batch of coloured clays each week. By labelling the bags that the clays are wrapped in with the colour and date on which it was made, you will always have a supply ready for use.

112

Colouring wet clay

This method mixes the stain into wet clay; use the same ratio of stain to clay as for the dry method.

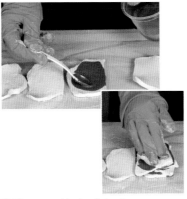

1 Mix the stain with water to form a thick cream consistency, then strain the mixture through a fine sieve into a small container.

2 Slice your block of clay into rough slabs with a cutting wire, then sandwich the coloured paste and clay in layers until all the mixture is used up.

3 Knead the clay until all the stain is thoroughly mixed through the clay and you have a uniform colour. This is messy, and it is best to avoid oxides and stains coming into contact with the skin, so wear rubber gloves.

113

Experimenting with laminated blocks

1 Laminated blocks (sliced from strips of layered coloured clays) can be put together in many combinations. A simple method is to arrange them to form a pattern in which the stripes spread in different directions.
Arrange the sections on a sheet of clean cotton fabric – better than plastic because the clay is usually sticky – which will absorb excess moisture but won't allow the clay to dry out too much.

2 Use a little water or slip and a fine brush to join the laminated sections together.

You can build patterns from laminated sections to any size you choose.

3 Once the pattern is complete, cover it with another sheet of fabric and roll it out using roller guides to keep the thickness of the slab even. Turn slabs through 90 degrees a few times when rolling out if you want to keep the pattern true and square. Failure to do this will distort the pattern but the results can be unexpectedly good.

The surface of agate forms can be scraped back very carefully with a metal kidney when almost dry, but this can be very tricky. Try sanding the surface after biscuit firing with fine-grained, wet-and-dry paper instead.

115

Appliqué

You can create appliqué surfaces by cutting shapes from thin agate slabs, then placing them on a backing slab and rolling them flush. This technique can create some very exciting surface patterns that you can use to make soft or hard slab forms or for moulding. For best results, the agate and backing slab should be the same consistency for a smooth join when rolled.

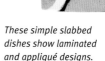

These simple slabbed dishes show laminated and appliqué designs.

Safety note

You should always wear a mask when sanding ceramic surfaces to avoid inhaling clay dust.

116

More ideas for ways to combine clays

Using up scraps
This is a great idea for using up spare scraps of clay – simply collect the scraps together and form them into a ball. Wedge the scraps together by twisting the ball in half then slapping the halves back together again. Repeat two or three times only, otherwise the colours will mix too much.

Reconstituted slabs
New slabs can be rolled from re-formed scraps and used as they are. Try cutting randomly shaped sections from the slab then rejoining them at different angles. After re-rolling you will have created another new slab.

Twisted coils
A great method for making larger sheets of agate is to roll a series of fat and thin coils (see page 72) of different-coloured clays. The coils can be twisted together before rolling out, or simply bunched together and rolled.

Stripes
Make stripes by twisting laminated strips into coils before rolling out. The lighter the twist, the wider apart the stripes will be.

Millefiore

Millefiore is made by rolling different coloured sheets of clay around a central coil to form concentric rings. The coils can then be cut into slices and reassembled.

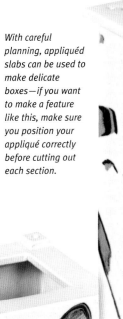

1 Arrange your pattern, using plenty of slip to seal the millefiore sections together. Don't worry that the slip obliterates the pattern; it will be revealed again later. You could also include laminated sections to make the pattern more interesting.

Millefiore patterns can be assembled in or over moulds to make bowls.

Tip: Soak your plaster mould in water for a couple of minutes before assembling millefiore – it will slow down the absorption of moisture from the clay, giving you time to finish putting all the sections together.

2 Once complete, leave the bowl to dry out to leather-hard, then carefully scrape away the joining slip with a metal kidney. Leave the bowl inside the mould to support it while you clean the inner surface because it is very fragile. Use fine steel wool as a final treatment to refine the surface and smooth out any irregularities. The same process can then be very carefully repeated on the outside of the bowl.

With careful planning, appliquéd slabs can be used to make delicate boxes—if you want to make a feature like this, make sure you position your appliqué correctly before cutting out each section.

TRY IT

118 **Thrown agate**

When used for throwing, agate will spiral up through the entire form. This technique is called neriage in Japan where it has been used for hundreds of years. (See pages 84–85 for the throwing technique.)

For the most subtle effect, mix only a small amount of coloured clay into your throwing clay. Limit the palette to one or two colours. You need only to make a sandwich of colour between the layers of base clay for throwing. Do not wedge them together, but take care to avoid air pockets. Make sure the base clay and coloured clay are the same consistency. Throw the form as directly as possible, using only a few lifts of the clay wall to keep the stripes bold. Don't worry if the form looks blurred after throwing. You will find the agate will emerge sharply when the form is turned.

SEE ALSO:
Ready-made clays,
  14–17
Preparing clay
  18–19

PINCHING

Pinching is one of the first techniques students learn at a pottery class because it helps to develop an understanding of clay and its working properties. It is a relatively simple technique – it is an instinctive way of handling the material – but nevertheless requires practice to perfect. In this section you will learn the basic making techniques and find lots of tips for success and development.

119 Before you begin – practical tips

- Hot hands dry clay out quickly, which can be a problem when pinching because it can cause cracking – the problem gets worse the more time you spend on a piece. The problem is simply remedied by cooling your hands under cold water periodically and working as quickly as possible.

- If you have never pinched before, use grogged clay – its greater strength means it will hold its shape without cracking. As you gain experience and a better understanding of how clay behaves you will be able to progress to smoother samples with finer particles that will pinch out to thinner sections.

- If you don't like the feel of grogged clay, try mixing it half-and-half with a smooth clay that fires to the same temperature – it will retain its strength for building but will also have a better surface quality and pinch out a little thinner.

- One of the biggest problems for pinchers is nails – they get in the way by cutting into the clay. If you can't bring yourself to keep them short, this is not the technique for you!

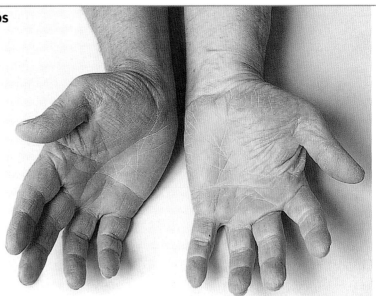

- A small amount of clay will pinch out a long way and this technique is not generally suitable for very large amounts – you will find you can increase the amount of clay you pinch as you gain experience. Start with an amount that will sit comfortably in the palm of your hand.

Pinch pot shapes

These cross-sections show the stages of making for three different types of pinch pot – deep, open/shallow and semicircular. The open form is by far the easiest to achieve when you first begin pinching but, as your understanding of the process grows, you will find you have more control and become able to perfect the others.

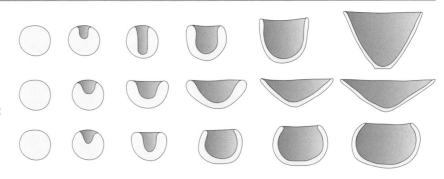

120

Pinching a basic shape

1 Form a small amount of well-prepared clay into a smooth ball that will fit into the palm of your hand. Press the thumb of your other hand down through the centre of the clay until you can feel some pressure in your palm. Measure the thickness at the base of the clay between your thumb and forefinger – it should be no thicker than 13 mm (1/2 inch). If you can't tell by feel, use a potter's pin to gauge the thickness. The hole made by the pin will quickly seal up again as you pinch out more.

2 Use your finger and thumb to pinch out the shape from the bottom of the ball first. Work in small, close pinching movements, rotating the clay in the palm of your hand with a rhythmic action to even out the marks made by your fingers. Keep the rim of the pot quite thick, and closed for as long as possible until you are ready to form the final shape. This will keep the wall from flaring out too quickly and becoming misshapen, torn or cracked.

FIX IT

121 **Pot uneven or floppy?**

• Pinch the wall upwards and outwards in stages. Work the whole form to one even thickness first, then again a little thinner and so on until you are happy with the shape.
• If the pot seems too floppy and won't hold its shape, dry the clay off a little inside and out with a hair dryer.

122

Making bases and facets

If you want your pot to have a defined base, turn the form over, then holding it very carefully, paddle the base into the required shape with a wooden spatula. You can paddle the walls in this way to change the shape of the whole pot, once it has been pinched to the correct size. Try paddling to make faceted-looking walls, perhaps starting with three sides and building up as you get more confident.

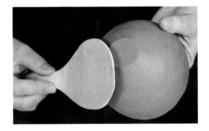

Remove any lumps and bumps from both the inner and outer surfaces of the pot using a metal scraper or kidney.

FIX IT

123 Rim too flared?

To correct the shape of a rim that has flared out too much or too soon, cut a series of "v"-shaped wedges from the walls of the form at even intervals. Draw the edges together and overlap them. If the clay has dried out significantly, score and slip the overlaps for a good seal.

Pinch the overlapped surfaces together until the wall is evened out to the same thickness. Blend and smooth the clay over as you work.

Make a small plastic rib from an old credit card to smooth and refine the inner wall of the pot. The rib can easily be cut to a suitable shape and size to use within the confined space.

---

124 Extensions

Extending the size of a pinch pot incorporates other techniques with the pinching process. Try out both methods shown here to see which you find easier.

Coiling on

1 You can use round or flattened coils for this method (see page 72). If the rim of the pot is very dry, score and slip before positioning the coil.

2 Pinch the coil in place as you fix it onto the rim. You can then blend the clay from the coil down onto the wall of the pot on the inside and the outside. Butt the two ends of the coil together, making sure they seal well without trapping air.

3 Pinch the coil upwards as you did for the main body of the pot, until the wall is the same thickness throughout. Scrape the walls to remove irregularities and smooth over the surface. You can add as many coils as you need in this way.

Pinching on

1 This technique uses flat sections of clay to increase size and height. It is useful for building up specific areas. Flatten small balls of clay by pinching out to roughly the same thickness as the wall of the pot. The pads of clay should be overlapped as they are pinched into place just inside the rim.

2 When adding pads of clay to build up the walls, smooth the surface with a scraper or kidney as you add each one. This will give you more control and allow you to develop the shape without having to make modifications later.

TRY IT

125 Making enclosed pinched forms

Many forms, from fruits and pods, to animals and sea creatures, to boxes and bottles, can be made from two joined pinched sections. Once you have mastered the technique of joining and manipulating, the possibilities for developing the form are endless.

1 Pinch two equally-sized semicircular pots, then score and slip both rims and join the two sections together. Hold the sections in place for a couple of minutes, applying light pressure to secure the join. When pinching the second half, check the size of the rim against the first one regularly to make sure they are the same size for a good fit. You will find it easier to pinch equally sized sections if you weigh the balls of clay to make sure they are the same size before you begin.

2 Reinforce the join of the form with a coil of soft clay. Use your finger or a modelling tool to blend it in thoroughly then smooth over the surface with a kidney. You will keep the shape of the form better if you support it in your hand as you reinforce the join – working on a board can distort the shape considerably.

126 Ideas for shaping enclosed forms

You need to take care when shaping enclosed pinched forms, but here are some ideas you can try.

The form can be shaped by paddling the walls with a wooden spatula – this has the added effect of smoothing the walls.

Use wooden blocks to create definite lines and indentations.

You can tap the form onto a board for a similar effect – this is helpful for getting the balance of a piece and helping you to decide how best it will sit.

You can achieve a softer finish simply by modelling with your fingers and thumbs – this gives scope to manipulate the shape in great detail.

SEE ALSO:
Ready-made clays,
14–17

Developing the shape

You can attach more pinched sections to a form to develop the shape or add sections made by other methods, depending on the effect you require. Use the following tips and techniques as a starting point to develop your own ideas.

 ## Small pinched additions

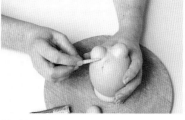

The technique
Pinch small amounts of clay to make features such as heads for figurative work, or to use as feet or lids. You will only be able to pinch such small amounts between one finger and thumb but the principles are the same as for larger amounts. The base of this pinched section has also been gently pulled to a point as a detail of the finished form.

Pinching feet
Pinch tiny balls, no bigger than a marble, to make feet. You will need three or more to hold a form securely. You can also cover the entire surface of pots with tiny balls like these for an unusual decorative finish – very retro!

Pinching lids
Lids can be pinched into all kinds of shapes to fit on bottles and boxes. Add textured coiled details as handles, or open out the shapes by carving sections out of the walls. The most important consideration when making lids like these is how they will locate onto the form. In this example you can see that a locating ring has been built up around the opening of the bottle form.

Pinched lids can easily be made to fit objects made by other methods, as in this case, where minaret shapes have been pinched and fitted onto thinly slabbed porcelain boxes.

FIX IT

 Unsure where to place sections?

Before joining extra sections, try them out at different angles on the body of the form to get the positioning right. You may have intended them for a particular place but you will often find they work better somewhere else. Mark the position before scoring and slipping to join.

Tip: Always reinforce additions with a coil of soft clay – the extra clay will allow you to blend over the join to make it look seamless.

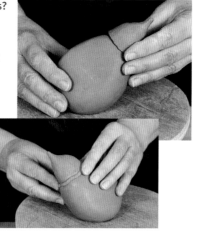

129

Slabbed additions

Slabbed details can be added to pinched forms successfully, providing the slab section is roughly the same as the body of the pot. After scoring, slipping and joining the sections, paddle them into place to ensure a good fit – this will also force out any air that may be trapped between the surfaces.

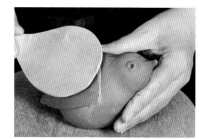

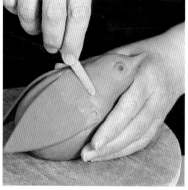

Where possible and appropriate, blend the edges of added slabs into the body to make them look less "joined on".

130

Coiled additions

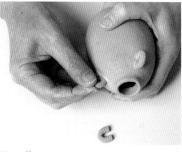

Handles

Use coils to make handles for pinch pots. They can be practical or purely decorative, as here. (See page 72.) Roll and form the coils into the required shape before joining them onto the pot. If you allow them to dry to the same stage as the body before attaching them you will ensure a secure fit.

Rims and footrings

Coils can be used to make decorative rims where they are left in their rounded form or blended in to form a locating ring for a lid. Foot rings can be made in the same way.

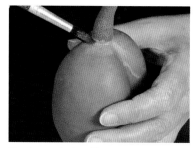

Sculptural details

Coils can be modelled to make details to add onto pinch pots like the stalk for this pod form. It is important to fix them to the body of your form very securely, reinforcing with tiny coils of soft clay whenever possible. If you want to texture your coil details do it before you fix them onto the form because they will be too fragile to texture once in place.

Support forms with fragile or delicate coiled additions on foam as they dry. To prevent the weight of the coil pulling away from the body, add some extra support underneath if required.

Decorative treatments for pinched forms

While many of the decorating techniques described throughout the book are perfectly appropriate for pinched forms, the following techniques are particularly suited to this method of making.

 132

Simple texturing with oxide wash

Forms are generally best textured before construction but this is not possible for pinched forms because of the making process. A simple texture can be created after making, using a serrated kidney or similar tool to score the surface. You will find that simple patterns can be created by scoring with serrated tools, but practise on scraps of clay first to find one that suits your form.

Textured surfaces like these look very organic and natural if simply covered with a thick oxide wash, which is then wiped back so that it only remains in the texture. The effects of oxides used in this way without glaze are very similar whichever one you choose – be it copper, cobalt, manganese or iron; most

 133

Paper resist for smoke firing

You can achieve wonderfully rich surface effects using masking tape to create patterns on the biscuit-fired pot. For best results the pot should be burnished (see page 127). The principle of this technique is that the masking tape is covered by a clay slurry before firing. The slurry acts as a resist to the smoke while the paper burns away to create the patterning.

are shades of dark when fired to high temperatures, so choose an inexpensive oxide to minimize waste.

Use the point of a wooden tool or even a pencil to stamp fine detail into the clay.

Tiny, squashed balls of clay carefully attached to surfaces have the effect of creating texture. Try stamping them for added detail.

Apply clay shapes over the surface to add natural details.

TRY IT

134 Masking tape patterns

1 Patterns can be achieved by tearing or cutting the masking tape into suitably sized strips. Use a cutting mat – the tape can be stuck onto the surface for cutting without any loss of adhesion later. Use a metal ruler and a heavy-duty craft knife to cut. Tear and cut as many strips as you think you will need before you begin and stick them onto the back of your hand for easy access as you work.

2 Patterns can be created quite randomly or in a very organized way using thin, cut strips of tape to delineate areas that are then filled in with torn strips. Build up the pattern carefully, leaving exposed areas between strips for the smoke to have maximum effect.

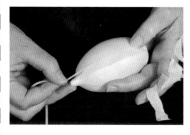

3 Carefully cut away areas of tape that overlap for a crisper effect. Use a sharp craft knife but take care not to cut into the surface of the pot.

4 Paint over the entire patterned area with slurry made from grogged clay. The slurry coat should be quite thick for best results – make sure you cannot see the clay surface through it but don't worry if you find that it does not cover the paper completely. Make grogged slurry by drying out your own clay then reconstituting it to make a thick slip. Just add a handful of sand or grog to the slip and mix well before use. Allow the slurry to dry off completely before firing in sawdust or newspaper (see page 31).

TRY IT

135 Experimental glazes

Experiment with low-firing brush-on glazes. They are available in the most amazing finishes – from vividly bright colours in matt or shiny varieties to artistic ranges with crystalline effects.

1 Brush a base colour glaze over the form, following the manufacturer's recommendations for good coverage.
2 Lightly sponge wax emulsion over the glazed surface using a very open-textured natural sponge.
3 Finally, sponge a contrasting colour over the waxed surface. The glaze will only stick where the wax did not form a resist.

• If you have access to a spray booth, try spraying the glazes instead of brushing them on – the effect will be similar but slightly more subtle.
• Experiment with glazes with different finishes – such as a shiny glaze over a matt base.
• Peruse the glaze catalogue and look for a few glazes that will combine to give many different finishes. You will find that a limited few, chosen for their colour compatibility, can create very exciting finishes.
• Forms decorated in this way will need to be supported on star stilts when firing if the whole surface has been glazed.

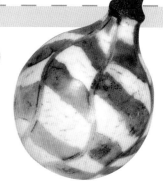

The fired pods show patterns made by torn and cut masking tape. The paper has burned away to create the pattern while the slurry has acted as a resist to the smoke. The stalks were left untreated to blacken completely.

SEE ALSO:
Ready-made clays,
14–17
Firing clay,
20–21

COILING

Coiling is perhaps the most versatile of the hand-building techniques, because it allows you to build forms of any design or scale. The tips on the following pages will help to speed up this usually slow and contemplative making process.

This Alan Foxley ribbed form shows the scale and potential of the coiling technique, given that the maker has a kiln large enough to fire the work.

136 Choosing clays for coiling

- Clay that is used for coiling must be "plastic" to keep it from cracking as you build the form.
- You may want the clay to be a rich colour that will complement your decorative finish. Remember that white-firing clays are the best choice for showing coloured glazes to their best advantage.
- Consider how the work will be fired. If it is to be fired and glazed in an electric kiln then you have the choice of many types of clay, but if it is to be fired in an extreme way, you should choose a clay that is specific to the technique – these are widely available from clay suppliers.

137 Round or flat coils?

Rounded coil

1 Roll to manageable lengths. If coils are too long, the shape becomes difficult to control. Coils are easily joined on the pot.
2 Roll coils with the palms of your hands to avoid making ridge marks with your fingers.
3 Don't roll the coils too thin – you will need enough clay to blend the coil on both sides when building the pot. A 2.5 cm (1 inch) diameter is a good thickness to work with.

Flattened coil

1 Roll coils for flattening a little thicker—they must have at least a 2.5 cm (1 inch) diameter.
2 Use the heel of the hand to flatten coils, not your fingers.
3 Elevate the coil at one end as you move along the length to flatten it.

This will keep it from sticking to the surface it is being flattened on.
4 For larger scale work, flatten bigger coils; the pot will build up much more quickly.
5 Always flatten coils on a sheet of plastic to prevent the clay sticking to the surface it is being flattened on. You can leave coils on the plastic sheet until positioned on the pot – this will help to keep the shape if you find it difficult to handle flattened coils. The plastic can be removed once the coil is secured.
6 To help form the shape of a pot, manipulate flattened coils into curves by turning the coil gently as it is flattened. This allows the form to be built up in either an inwards or outwards direction.

The term "rounded coil" describes the coil as it is originally rolled. Coils vary in size, from thin for very fine building to more than 2.5 cm (1 in) thick for larger-scale work.

A flattened coil is simply a large, rounded coil that has been flattened out with the hand. Working with flattened coils will generally speed up the making process. It is similar in many ways to the slabbing process.

138

Rolling the perfect coil

Roughly form the clay into a thick sausage shape and then, working on a non-absorbent surface, roll the coil using the palms of your hands – not your fingers – to avoid making unnecessary marks in the coil.

139

Rounding a flattened coil

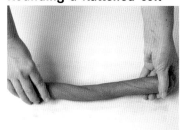

Coils almost always flatten in the rolling process. To bring them back to a rounded shape, hold the coil at each end and twist in opposite directions. Then re-roll the coil to remove the twist marks. This can be done as often as necessary and will give the coil added strength.

TRY IT

141 **Making extruded coils**

To make coils for surface decoration, use a mini hand-extruder. These are widely available from pottery suppliers, are relatively cheap, and come with a set of dies for different-sized coils and other shapes. See page 76 for ways to use this type of coil.

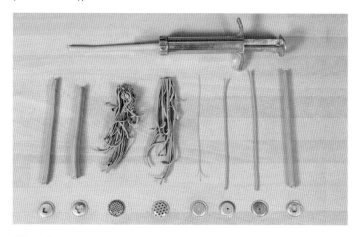

140

Stylizing flattened coils

Use this type of coil over moulds to make woven forms (see page 80). The patterned side of the coil can form the top or underside of the form, depending on the shape. You can also use these coils to make decorative rims for your work. Attach them to pinched, slabbed or coiled forms – the secret to success is simply to make sure the coil is the same thickness as the wall of the pot it is being added to.

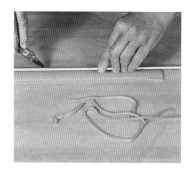

Shape the coils
Use a roller guide to shape the coil into a slightly domed shape by placing it over the surface and then applying pressure at each edge. Cut away the surplus clay to neaten the edges.

Add surface decoration
Use the side of the roller guide to make grooves in the coil and small stamps to create surface decoration – pen tops make good stamps for small-scale work – look out for interesting shaped ones.

SEE ALSO:
Developing ideas,
34–35
Developing form,
36–37

Formers and templates

Before you start to build your coil pot you should know what shape you intend to build – this may seem an obvious point to make, but people start to coil with no real idea of the intended shape, and their pots will look unresolved as a result. Pages 146–151 will give you lots of outline ideas if you can't make up your mind.

 142

Making an outline former

Making an outline former will help you to keep control of the shape as you build it. The best material to make the former from is thin MDF, which can easily be cut with a strong knife; thick cardboard or hardboard also work well.

Resist Raku vessel made using an outline former to control the shape.

FIX IT

 143 **Making a former?
Things to bear in mind:**

The board should be large enough to allow you to hold it comfortably when it is in use. Take a rough measurement by gripping the side of the board before drawing and cutting out the shape. Draw the outline shape with a black marker pen – it is easier to see than a pencil line when cutting out.

The board must have a level base so that it can sit on the board that the pot is made on – this will keep the shape true.

To use the former, hold it flat on the board the pot is sitting on, then draw carefully around the form to check the shape. It will help if the board is sitting on a whirler when you do this. Make any necessary corrections to the shape as soon as you detect them.

TRY IT

 144 **Different base forms**

Slabbed base (right): Cut the base from a soft slab so that the clay will be easy to blend in when the coil is added on. Make the base a little larger than required, because some size will be lost when the first coil is attached.

Pinched base (above): Pinch out the base shape of your pot (see page 64). Pinch the shape by small degrees, using your outline former regularly to check that the shape is correct. Make sure that the base is large enough to support the size of the pot you are making – if it is too small, the pot will topple over easily.

Create a foot ring: Simply place a small disc on the underside of the base slab. The disc can be purpose-made from biscuit-fired clay, or you could use a large coin or flat button.

Complicated constructions

By building with coils of different profiles, or by changing the shape of the form as you build your pot, you open up an infinite range of creative possibilities.

145

Building with flattened coils

1 Before you begin, score and slip the outer edge of the base with a toothbrush and a little water. When using flattened coils you should score and slip each coil before joining the next one on.

2 Manipulate the form – placing the inner, concave side of a curved coil onto the base allows the form to curve outwards.

Tip

Keep checking the shape. To help keep the shape of the pot regular, use a blade to level the top of each coil after it has been attached and reinforced – before adding the next coil. Remember to use your outliner former at regular intervals (preferably after each coil has been joined) to keep the shape of the pot looking good.

3 Reinforce all joins, both inside and out, with thin coils of soft clay. These should be blended in well with a wooden tool before being scraped back with a metal kidney to define the shape and remove excess clay.

4 Once the first coil has been secured in place on the inside, turn the shape over and blend the base down onto the wall of the pot. You can remove the disc from the underside at this stage if you want.

5 To join coils, overlap the ends where they meet, then cut through both sections diagonally. Remove the surplus before joining the cut ends together carefully, making sure they are secure and that no air is trapped in the join.

146

Building with rounded coils

The principles of building with rounded coils are the same whether you are beginning from a slabbed or a pinched base.

1 Score and slip the base before you attach the first coil. This will not be necessary thereafter if the clay is soft enough to blend in, but for pinched bases especially, it is advisable.

2 The form must be supported on the underside as you blend the coil onto the base. Blend the clay downwards using your thumb, finger or a wooden tool.

3 When the coil has been blended in on the inside of the form, turn it over and repeat the blending process on the outside, taking care not to squash the form.

4 Overlap and cut through the coils diagonally (as for flattened coils) before joining the ends together and blending in well. You can join more than one coil at a time in this way, or simply continue to build the shape for the length of the coil – winding it around until it is used up. Do make sure the coils are blended together very well if you are applying more than one, and check the shape regularly against your outline former.

Paddle the surface
Use a wooden spatula to paddle the surface of the pot – this will help to compact the clay and ease out any surface irregularities.

147

Making shape changes

Round to oval
Change a shape from round to oval by simply squeezing the walls gently between both hands then paddling the surface to refine the shape.

This paper resist, smoke-fired vessel was built in the round then altered when almost complete to create the narrowed neck and elliptical rim.

Concave/convex
Make an elliptical rim and use a blade to shave the clay away so that the wall is convex on one side and concave on the other – this will create a form with a back and a front.

148

Decorative techniques to try

To narrow a square neck further, cut away v-shaped sections from the pre-shaped corners, then join the clay back together with slip. Reinforce them with coils of soft clay for a good join.

Create interesting and organic surface qualities using a serrated kidney to texture the clay. This type of kidney can make many surface patterns – here it has been used in a crosshatch style – but it is a good idea to experiment on spare clay first.

Coiling on from an irregular-shaped rim will radically change the look of a pot and give it a very organic look. Work out the shape of the rim using a pointed tool to mark it out first – when you are happy with the shape, cut the excess clay away from the rim with a craft knife. When you coil onto the rim again, work the coils in a different direction for best effect.

Scoring the clay with a knife is a simple but effective decorative technique – it works well in contrast to the crosshatched body of this vessel and both finishes add to the organic look of the form.

FIX IT

149 **Need to change the shape of the pot?**

Provided that your clay is still in a soft enough state to be manipulated, you can change the shape of your pot at any stage by cutting the required shape from the wall then joining the edges back together and reinforcing both the inside and outside with coils of soft clay.

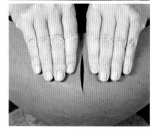

This form by Audrey Richardson has a double elliptical rim making both sides equally balanced, but it has the effect of making the form seem round when it is in fact very slim.

Round to square
Change a shape from round to square by placing two splayed fingers inside the rim and paddling the wall into shape. Repeat this three times until the rim is roughly squared, then repeat the process once more to make any fine adjustments to the shape.

SEE ALSO:
Improvising tools,
26–27

Useful tools for awkward angles

Scraping tools with different rounded edges are especially good for the insides of pots in which there may be angles that are hard to reach.

Ribs

Wooden and bamboo ribs are available in lots of different shapes – you should only need one or two, but look out for ones that have several functions, including a straight edge, a point, a curve and a rounded edge.

Useful for walls where there is a straight edge – good for scraping and smoothing.

A very useful shape with a rounded end, a straight edge, a curved edge and a point.

A good shape where awkward angles are hard to reach.

This rib has a useful shape cut from one end, perfect for finishing rims smoothly.

A bamboo version of no. 3 but curved, making it even more versatile.

Loop tools

Loop tools are also useful for removing excess clay to reduce the thickness of walls – a large loop that is rounded at one end and pointed at the other is the best choice for the inside of larger coiled pots.

This very useful tool came in an inexpensive pack of children's craft tools.

A loop tool has a big loop; rounded at one end, pointed at the other.

Wooden kitchen tools can be useful – look for ones with unusual shapes.

FIX IT

 Can't reach awkward angles?

Make your own tools – for awkward angles inside pots this is often the best solution, when standard tools are just not quite right (for more information, see pages 26–27).

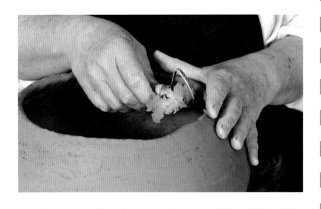

Finishing the inside rim of a large pot with a homemade loop tool.

SEE ALSO:
Agate,
60–61

Decorative ways to use coils

You can use coils very creatively for decorative effects. The following techniques show just how versatile this making method can be, given that all the bowls start off as basically the same shape.

The finished bowl, before firing. It can be simply fired up to the clay's top temperature without glaze, or a transparent glaze could be applied either to the inside only, or all over.

151 Coiling into moulds

1 Start by inserting a disc of plain porcelain into the bottom of the mould to form the base.

2 Position the textured coils in alternate coloured rows around the porcelain base section inside the mould.

3 After several rows, carefully overlay the pattern with thin slabs of plain porcelain to form a lining and bind the coils together. Press the lining into place, taking care not to trap air. Smooth over with a kidney to finish.

4 Continue to build up the pattern to the top of the mould, then finish lining it to the top.

FIX IT

152 Coils breaking in the mould?

Porcelain dries out much faster than any other clay, which means you have to work fast for best results. This is even more vital when you are working with porcelain in a plaster mould. The clay must be soft for this technique – to keep your coils soft enough to work successfully, spray them with a mist of water before placing them in the mould.

TRY IT

153 Making coil-rolling easy

• Textured rubber bath or draining-board mats are great for rolling coils on to create interesting surface qualities; purpose-made ones are also available from pottery suppliers.
• Roll thin coils on a non-absorbent board for this technique before finally rolling them lightly over the textured mat.
• Roll more coils than you think you will need before you begin to construct the pot. Keep them wrapped in plastic until you are ready to use them, because porcelain dries out exceptionally quickly.

154

A plaiting technique

1 Insert a slabbed base section in the mould then position the first plait. Blend the bottom of the plait onto the base with a finger to secure it.

The finished, unfired bowl (below). Suggestions for decoration:

• A simple, coloured glaze will accentuate the pattern of the plaits.

• Oxide wash works well with or without a glaze over the top. If you want to glaze over the oxide choose an opaque one rather than transparent it will accentuate the pattern better.

• Try out some of the brush-on glazes available from most pottery suppliers. They come in a myriad of finishes and can produce some very exciting results. These are usually most suited for decorative ware, so ask for advice on the best ones for domestic ware.

2 Fix the plaits at intervals around the pot to begin with – this will help you to space them correctly. You can roughly break off the plaits at the top of the mould with a finger, or cut them with a knife. When they are all in place, blend the plaits together carefully – this will squash the clay into the wall of the mould, but the plaited pattern will remain. Try not to distort the clay too much, however. You can add a flattened coil to extend the size of the bowl once it is out of the mould if you choose.

Tips

• Choose soft, "plastic" clay for this technique.
• Roll the coils quite thin for best effect, and make them as long as possible, because quite a lot of the length is lost in the plaiting process.
• Make all the plaits you will need before you start, because the mould will dry out the clay very quickly once you begin. Stopping to make more plaits halfway through the construction process would cause discrepancies during drying and may result in cracks.
• Keep the plaits wrapped in plastic until you are ready to start building.

FIX IT

155 **Plaits won't fit evenly in the mould?**

Try scaling the size of the plaits up or down. There will always be a problem when fitting plaits into a mould that flares outwards, because it is narrower at the bottom than the top. You can position intermediate plaits slightly higher than the base as an alternative – just make sure they fit neatly between those on either side, and that you blend them in well.

Bits of white clay contaminating the surface?

This is a problem when working with such contrasting colours of clay. Try removing them carefully with a pin or similar tool, then smoothing over the area with a kidney. You can also wait until the pot has been biscuit-fired, then sand the offending spot with some fine wet-and-dry sandpaper to remove it. Wear a mask if you choose this method, to avoid inhaling clay dust.

156

Decorating with extruded coils

Choose a small-holed die to make the coils, and only extrude the amount you need at any one time. These coils dry out quickly so must be used immediately, as they are extruded. You'll need to use really soft clay to be able to extrude it.

1 Moisten the surface of the pot slightly with a damp sponge in the area where the coil is to be applied. Repeat this as each new coil is attached. Carefully lay the coils over the moist surface to create your pattern.

2 Use a printing roller or small rolling pin to carefully roll the coils onto the surface. You will find the coils spread out as they are rolled, which is why they need to be thin; they also distort a little, but this adds to the character of the design.

3 You can add additional features such as tiny balls of clay if you wish—roll these in the same way as the coils, and texture them with small stamps for extra effect.

The finished, unfired bowl (left).
Suggestions for decoration:
Simple transparent glaze is the best decoration for work of this type. Try a transparent, colored glaze for a slightly different effect—it will color the white pattern but not have too much effect on the red body.

157

A raised coil surface

This technique is very similar to decorating with extruded coils, except that the coils are rolled instead, and are much bigger. Apply coils to the surface and paddle them flat.

Make the rim
When the surface is entirely covered, apply several coils to make a decorative rim. Blend these in on the inside of the form only, and paddle the outside gently so that the coils look the same as the decorative ones.

The finished, unfired bowl.
Suggestions for decoration:
Any glaze will work because the coils stand in relief, creating shadows. You could try oxide washes with or without glaze, or apply sponged or stamped luster or enamel decoration to the raised coils after glaze-firing to bring them into focus and add depth.

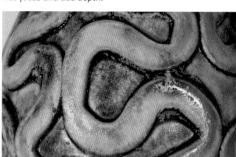

158

Sectional coiling

This technique requires you to put small decorative sections or panels together before building the pot. It is a slightly difficult technique to master. A good tip is to coil a base for the pot before you begin, and measure the circumference so that you can work out how many sections you will need to fit around it, and how large each section needs to be.

1 Roll out a good supply of fairly thin coils – no bigger than 6 mm (1/4 in) diameter – and keep them under plastic until you are ready to use them. Next, start to make your panels to your chosen design. The ones shown here are being interlocked into arches. Make as many sections as you think you will need before starting to construct the form – keep them under plastic after putting them together.

2 Score and slip the rim of the base, then position the first two panels on the rim, ensuring that they adhere to the surface. Fill in the space between the panels with more coils to build the pattern up.

3 After attaching two panels and filling in the space in between them, blend the coils together on the inside carefully, supporting the form on the outside with your other hand. Continue to build the form in this way to the required size. Once the first level is complete you can add a second level and so on, but if the form bellies out you will need to increase the size of the panels by one coil at each level. Add a flattened coil rim to finish.

The finished, unfired bowl. Suggestions for decoration:
Any of the previously mentioned glazing or oxide wash techniques will look good on this surface. You could also try applying a dark-coloured glaze, then wiping it back on the outside so that it remains in the texture only. You could apply another, lighter or transparent glaze over the outer surface so that the pattern would still show through.

FIX IT

159 **Coils separating when you blend them on the inside?**

The most probable cause is that the clay is too dry, making the coils hard to blend. Try using softer clay. Alternately, try blending the coil panels together before fitting them onto the pot. This will have the effect of squashing the pattern a little but should make them more secure. To make the rest of the pot look the same once the spaces between the panels have been filled in, paddle the outside gently with a wooden spatula. Make sure you support the outside sufficiently as you blend on the inside.

Decorative coils shrunk away from holes?

This problem arises when the clay of the body of the pot and the clay of the decorative coils are at a different stage of dryness. This means they will shrink at different rates and create tension. If this happens at the green stage, try making a thick slip from the same dry powdered clay reconstituted with distilled vinegar. Fill in the cracks with the slip, then smooth over carefully. If it happens after biscuit firing, try using the magic mixture on page 128 to solve the problem.

160

A cut and fill technique

This technique uses patterned coils to fill in cutaway areas in a pre-coiled form.

1 Score and slip the openings of the holes before fitting the decorative coils in place. Blend the coils into the body of the pot on the inside while supporting the outside, then scrape away the excess on the inside so that the wall is smooth and even. The top coil should extend above the rim.

2 When all the holes have been filled in, build up the rim with more coils. Position the coils between the raised pattern and place one more over the top to finish. Blend them in well on the inside and scrape back the surface to neaten it. If you want to level the top, simply paddle it a little with a wooden spatula.

Tips

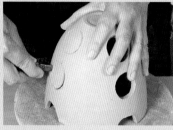

Using biscuit- or pastry-cutters as markers will help to make sure that the size of the cut out sections is always the same. Don't cut any of the holes until you have spaced them all correctly – simply mark the holes with a pointed tool, then if one is out of line you can smooth over the clay and reposition it.

Cut all the holes before you begin to fill them back in – this will ensure you get the spacing correct.

Cutting semicircles at the rim of the form will allow you to extend the design for a decorative effect.

Make the decorative coils and allow them to dry to the same stage as the body of the pot before fixing them in place. You will need to measure them against the holes as you make them – they should be slightly larger for a good fit – this will allow for shrinkage in the drying and firing process.

The finished, unfired bowl. Suggestions for decoration: Any of the previously mentioned decorative techniques would work well. You can try Raku firing with a turquoise lustre or a white crackle glaze. You could accentuate the decorative coils by waxing over them before glazing, so that after firing they are black from carbonization, in contrast to the rest of the body.

SEE ALSO:
Ready-made clays,
14–17

THROWING

Throwing is arguably the most difficult making technique to master. The fundamental key to success is practice, but often the most simple tip – such as being shown the correct hand position – will revolutionize your understanding of a process and make the difference for early success. This section is full of essential tips and information to start you off throwing.

The simplicity of this thrown form is balanced by the restrained glaze.

161 Right clay, right result

It is essential to choose the right clay for the type of work you are considering. Clay for throwing should have good plasticity (the ability to retain its shape when worked, to produce a smooth and unbroken surface) but must also meet your requirements in terms of temperature, fired colour, strength and texture. Before buying your clay, ask yourself the following questions:

• What do I want to make?
• Will it be functional or nonfunctional?

• Is it for indoors or outdoors?

As a general rule:
• **Smooth clay** is used for smaller or delicate ware.
• **Medium-textured clay** is used for tableware, ovenware and larger pots.
• **Coarse clay** is used to make garden pots, or pots that need to withstand thermal shock (as in Raku firing, for example – see page 30).

All these clay types are available as "earthenware" or "stoneware".

TRY IT

163 Crack-resistant clay

If you generally like the qualities of the clay you have chosen, but find that it does not have enough wet strength, try adding 8–10 per cent fine sand or grog (40–90 mesh). This will greatly improve its throwing properties while only marginally affecting plasticity, and will have the added benefits of making the body more crack-resistant and reducing warping.

162 What type of surface?

The type of surface treatment you want is an important consideration when choosing your clay.

• Colourful slips or glazes generally appear brighter on a white clay body. The exception is if you are using the "Majolica" technique of painting oxides or body stains over a white tin glaze. This works best over a red earthenware body where the effect is softened by the interaction of glaze with iron in the clay.
• Colours are brightest at lower temperatures (earthenware); however earthenware for domestic use is not as durable as the stoneware equivalent.
• Some clays (especially iron-loaded varieties) are designed to react with glaze treatments to give specific surface results such as iron spots. Do not choose this type of clay unless you want this effect!

• Work that is intended to be placed outdoors will need a clay body that will fire to "vitrification" (stoneware) to avoid damage from weather. Generally a coarser, firmer clay is required to hold larger shapes, but these can be hard for the beginner to throw so don't start off with this type of clay.
• Consider glaze safety – some glaze ingredients, such as lead (even in fritted form) are considered unsafe for domestic use. But generally, the higher the temperature at which the clay is fired, the safer it is, because the body and glaze "vitrify" and prevent absorption or leaching of any component ingredients.

The wheel head for your needs

A modern potter's wheel is a totally controllable piece of machinery – usually electronically powered – for which there is often a choice of wheel head to meet your specific needs. The basic wheel head is a simple disc etched with concentric lines designed to help centre clay for throwing and pots for trimming. Wheel heads are available in several sizes. It is not essential to have more than one size unless you are production throwing. For most purposes, a larger head would be the most useful.

Accommodating wooden bats
This wheel head (right) is specially designed for use with wooden bats. The cutout sections at the sides of the wheel head allow the bats to be lifted with ease while the pot is still in position, to avoiding distortion of the piece through handling. Ask your pottery supplier about this type of wheel head – most wheel manufacturers have their own version designed for locating wooden bats.

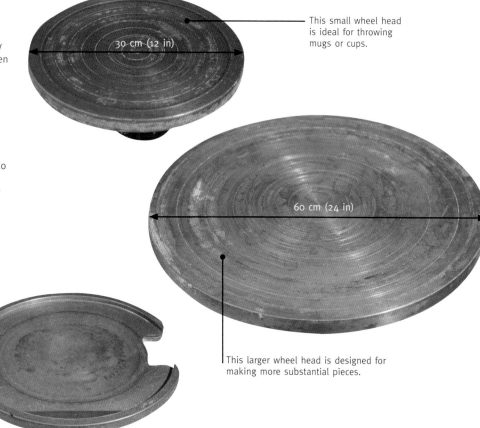

30 cm (12 in)

This small wheel head is ideal for throwing mugs or cups.

60 cm (24 in)

This larger wheel head is designed for making more substantial pieces.

Preparation of clay for throwing success

The preparation of clay for throwing is more important than for any other method of making. Consistency and softness are vital – therefore the clay should be wedged and kneaded to remove all inconsistencies, variations in hardness and air bubbles (see pages 18–19).

As a beginner, you will find it easier to centre soft clay, but if it is too soft it will struggle to hold its shape as you pull the wall up during the throwing process.

By contrast, if the clay is too hard you will have to apply greater strength to centre it and more pressure to shape the form, which could lead to twisting, warping or even cracking. It is generally considered best to begin with a softer clay to master the initial centring technique then, as you become more confident, you can progress to firmer clay for larger pieces of work.

Once you have kneaded your clay, form it into suitably-sized balls for the pots you want to throw, then store these under plastic sheeting to prevent moisture evaporation until you are ready to throw them.

Storing prepared clay

Store your prepared clay balls in a plastic bowl – it keeps them contained and gives you more space. Cover the bowl with a sheet of plastic.

TRY IT

166 Making your own bats

• If you want to make your own bats, try making them from 6-mm (¼-in) Perspex instead of marine ply (which can be very expensive). Look in the offcut bins in plastics shops for cheap Perspex. To improve the grip, scour the high-gloss surface with glasspaper while the bat is rotating on the wheel.
• You can also make bats from clay fired at a high temperature: make them about 19 mm (¾ in) thick and dry them between boards to keep them flat before firing.

Setting up your workspace

Before you start to throw it's important to prepare your workspace, making sure that everything that you need is handy.

SEE ALSO:

Basic tools,
22–25
Improvising tools,
26–27

Keeping things handy

Position the wheel adjacent to some shelving so that you can easily move your work across as you finish it. Place a table next to the wheel; use this to store clay and tools for easy access, and to provide an extra surface for pots as you make them. The water bowl should fit into a corner of the pan so as not to get in the way, and hang hand towels close by.

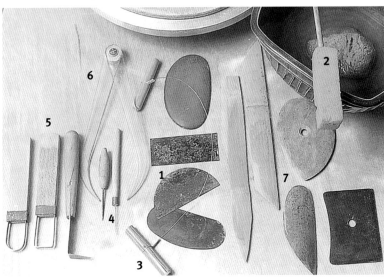

Protective clothing

There are conflicting opinions about the type of protective clothing that is best for clay work. Cotton overalls or aprons are the traditional choice, but these absorb clay, and as it dries it forms dust that may be inhaled. Cotton also offers no protection from water. Nylon alternatives are waterproof and will protect you from heavy soiling but there is some suggestion that they create as much dust because any dried clay brushes off more readily. The best solution is to wash whichever type you choose often to minimize the dangers. It is advisable to wear short sleeves when throwing to keep your hands and arms unhindered.

Beginner's throwing kit

See the image below left.

FOR CLAY PREPARATION
1 Bench scraper/kidney
Use a bench scraper to remove excess clay.

FOR THROWING
2 Sponges
Use sponges for mopping up water and applying water to rims during the throwing process. A sponge on a stick is useful for removing excess water from inside the bottoms of tall pots.

3 Cutting wire
Use cutting wire for cutting pots off the wheel head, trimming rims and decorative techniques such as faceting. Several strands of thick wire wound together make deep decorative marks on the bottoms of pots.

4 Potter's pin/needle
A potter's pin is useful for testing the thickness of bases when throwing. You can also use it to remove excess clay from rims to even them up, or to eliminate air bubbles that have not been removed in the wedging process.

5 Potter's knife
A potter's knife is a useful tool for removing excess clay from rims and releasing wooden bats from the wheel head.

6 Calipers
Use calipers for measuring diameters when you are making multipart pots, and to ensure well-fitting lids.

7 Selection of ribs
Traditionally ribs were made from wood or bamboo, but they are now also available in plastic or metal. They help to pull up the walls of pots and compact the bases of plates and other open forms.

169

Ideas to make things easier

Place all your tools on a rubber mat (the type used in sinks and showers) next to or on the wheel shelf. You will find it much easier to lift them from this with wet hands and they won't stick to the surface when you put them down again.

Small tool tidy

A tool tidy (below right) that fits onto your wheel shelf will contain small items that easily get lost when throwing. Make it to any size by cutting a section of firm foam, then sticking this down onto a piece of wooden batten with waterproof glue. Add a piece of rigid plastic tubing filled with sponge at one end of the batten, then glue two shelf clips to the underside. This gadget will hold kidneys, ribs and other small tools, and the tube is great for potter's pins.

Custom steel tools

Metal engineers (find one in the phone book or online) can cut stainless steel tools of almost any shape. These tools will last much longer than the wooden varieties and will not rust like many commercially bought tools.

A selection of stainless steel tools for throwing

To keep larger tools tidy and do your bit for recycling, cut the bottom end off a plastic bottle, leaving the lid in place at the top. Fix a shelf clip or hook some sturdy wire through the bottle, close to the open end, then fit it over the slip tray. It will contain calipers and sponge mops, or any other large tools you may use. Any water or clay slurry that accumulates can be released simply by unscrewing the cap.

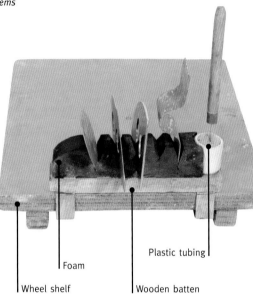

Foam

Plastic tubing

Wheel shelf

Wooden batten

170

Practicalities

- How you work will be dictated by practical things such as the size of your working space, how much shelf space you have to contain your work, the firing capacity and upper temperature of your kiln, and even your ability to sit at the wheel for a length of time.

- Throwing can generate a lot of work in a short space of time that you will need to accommodate. Work out how much you can comfortably make to fill the available space, bearing in mind the capacity of your kiln.

- Whether seated or standing, a good throwing position is important for success. The upper part of the body must be able to lean over the wheel head to give support to the arms and hands. Most seated wheels are adjustable; if yours is not, find a stool or chair that will allow you to work at the correct angle. If you prefer to stand, a low step can be useful to raise yourself to the correct height.

- If you have a back problem, be aware that you will probably be sitting for long periods when throwing. Remember to straighten your back periodically or get up and do something different from time to time to avoid exacerbating the problem.

- Throwing can be quite messy – try to contain the area in which you work to make cleaning easier and clean up after each session to minimize mess.

SEE ALSO:
Setting up your
workspace,
86–87

Centring the clay

You can achieve nothing on a wheel until you can centre
the clay. From the basic hand position through to fully
centred clay, this section will take you through all
the key stages of this most important technique.

171
Positioning the clay on the wheel

1 The wheel head must be clean,
dust-free, and moist in order for the
clay to adhere to it. Wipe over the
surface with a damp sponge – don't
use excessive water, or the clay
will slide off the wheel head as it
gathers speed.

2 The wheel should be spinning at
speed as you centre the clay, but slow
it down to open out and lift the walls.
Try not to spend too long centring
the clay or you will overwork it,
but do take the time to perfect the
centring technique before moving
onto the next stage.

3 Brace your left arm on the side of
the pan. This hand controls the side
of the clay. Your right forearm should
also be braced on the pan to allow
the edge of your hand to control the
top of the clay. Keep your back and
shoulders rigid, with your elbows
tucked into your body for support.

Centring a cone
*Forming the clay ball into a cone shape
prior to positioning it on the wheel makes
it easier to position correctly and will help
the centring process. Position the cone at the
centre of the wheel, then strike it with
the palm of your hand to fix it in place.*

The perfect hand position
*Here you can see the hands in place
without clay to give a clear idea of their
correct positions. Your hands should be
braced against one another at this stage
of the process.*

Staying dry

You will need to use water for lubrication when throwing – the clay should slide easily through your hands without dragging or sticking. Try not to use too much, though, because it will make the clay soft and flabby.

One of the most irritating problems when throwing is water running down your arms! Overcome this by wearing sport wristbands to soak up the water.

Use the rings

Use the concentric rings on the wheel head to help you position the clay as close to the centre as possible.

FIX IT

173 Common problems

- **The clay has not stuck to the wheel head:** Either the wheel head or the clay ball was too wet – both should be just damp.
- **The clay twists and tears away from the wheel:** You are not using enough water – it is a fine balance between too much and too little.
- **The rim seems to be centred but the body of the form is not:** You are not applying enough pressure with the hand that controls the side of the clay – it needs to be held more rigidly. Make sure your hands are braced correctly against one another.
- **The clay refuses to centre:** It may be too hard – try wedging some softer clay into the ball (see page 18). Alternatively, try tucking your elbow into your stomach so that you can use your body weight to help push your left hand against the clay. Sometimes it helps to close your eyes so that you are feeling rather than seeing the clay.

172
Centring any weight of clay

1 The following technique will allow you to centre any weight of clay once it is positioned on the wheel. Set the wheel spinning and dribble a small amount of water over the clay.

2 Apply pressure with your left hand on the side of the clay so that it rises as it rotates.

3 Now apply pressure with the side of your right hand on top of the clay while gently relaxing the pressure from your left hand. The clay will go down. It is this up and down movement while the clay is rotating that gently eases it into the centre. You may need to repeat the process several times before you get it right.

Look, no hands!
The clay is centred when it runs smoothly through your hands with no wobbles. It is vitally important that you take your hands away from the centred clay gently because it can easily be knocked off centre by jerky movements.

174
Methodical practice

Prepare six balls of soft clay, increasing the weight of each by 227 g (1/2 lb) and beginning at a weight you feel comfortable with. Prepare six more balls of slightly firmer clay in the same way. Then prepare six more balls of even firmer clay. Practise centring the soft balls of clay until you feel confident with the technique, then move on to the slightly firmer clay, and so on until you have used all the balls. By repeating the process and working methodically you will quickly learn what differences in clay quality and weight make to centring. And remember: clay is never wasted – it can always be recycled (see page 18).

SEE ALSO:
Setting up
your workspace,
86–87

Opening up

"Opening up" is not a call to confess all, but the next stage in the throwing process. This is the term used to describe the technique of making an opening in the centred ball of clay to begin to form the wall and base of a pot.

175

Start with the thumb

Place the flat of your right thumb over the centre of the clay and place the fingers of your left hand on the thumb for added pressure. Push your thumb into the clay so that the ball opens up into a doughnut shape.

This will allow you to see inside and judge the depth, and will help to prevent you knocking the clay off centre. Don't try to open up the clay by creating a vertical hole down through the centre – keep your thumb flat! Remember to lubricate the clay from time to time.

Getting the base thickness right

Foot rings are not generally turned on basic cylinder shapes; therefore the thickness at the base should be equal to the thickness of the wall when the form is fully thrown. For small cylinders, a 5 mm (1/4 in) thickness at the base is ample – allow too much and the pot will be heavy and lose height. If the cylinder is to be adapted to a bellied-out form, you can leave a greater thickness at the base to allow a foot ring to be turned later.

Before lifting the walls of your cylinder it is important to measure the thickness of the clay at the base.

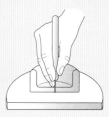

To do this, push a pin through the clay until it meets the wheel head, then run your finger down the pin till it meets the clay. Remove the pin with your finger still in place and you will be able to see the thickness. If it is too thick, repeat the opening up process.

Height x width	Base thickness
150 x 100 mm (6 x 4 in)	5 mm (1/4 in)
300 x 120 mm (12 x 5 in)	12 mm (1/2 in)
150 x 200 mm (6 x 8 in)	5 mm (1/4 in)

Base thickness

6
4

12
5

6
8

176

Three essential hand positions for opening up

1 With the first finger of your left hand inside and your thumb on the outside of the clay wall – pinching like a crab's claw – gently squeeze and lift the wall up a couple of centimetres or so.

2 Now place your right hand on the outside of the form and continue to lift the form upwards and inwards. Your right hand prevents the clay from naturally opening out. You should be aiming to keep the base broad and the top narrow.

3 When you have completed the first lift, check that the top is running true. You can consolidate by carefully holding the rim between the fingers of your left hand, while gently applying pressure with the fingers of your right. You should do this after each lift. If there is excessive unevenness, remove the rim with a pin or wire.

177

A strong base

It is vitally important to compress the clay in the base of the pot by running your thumb over the surface from the centre to the outside edge three times to prevent the base from cracking. Alternatively, you could use a knuckle, sponge or rib to compress the base. Using the same thumb positions, open up the form by applying pressure across the base to the side, bending the thumb of your right hand from the flat position as you reach the edge, to help shape the wall.

The base of your pot can be smoothed flat with a rib as it is compressed, or alternatively, the marks made by the action can be left as a feature providing they are not so deep that they create a very uneven section.

FIX IT

178 **Removing clay from rims**

• **Using a potter's pin:** With the wheel rotating slowly, hold the pin steadily at the required point then lift the excess clay away with your other hand.

• **Using a cutting wire:** Again, with the wheel rotating slowly, brace a section of the wire between the thumbs of both hands then cut through the clay wall at the relevant point. Lift the excess off quickly but carefully with the wire.

Knuckling up and lifting off

Knuckling up is critical to the success of lifting the clay smoothly and efficiently into a cylinder.

 179

Foolproof knuckling up

1 When you start knuckling up, the position of your thumb and finger is critical. Your right forefinger should wrap around the top of your thumb, as shown here.

2 Place your knuckle against the outside edge of the form and the fingers of your left hand inside it, so that the clay is trapped between them. The thumb of your left hand should rest on the knuckled hand.

3 Keeping your hands in this position, lift the clay gently to form a basic cylinder shape. Repeat this action as many times as necessary to lift the shape to the required height.

4 Once you have finished lifting the clay, and before removing your fingers and knuckle, it is important to relax and allow the shape of the top to come back to round. If you remove the knuckle too quickly, the shape will be knocked off centre and the form will have a wobble.

 180

Keeping your work tidy

Mopping out
Mop up water from the inside of the pot with a sponge at regular intervals to prevent saturation of the base. If your hand will not reach inside to the base, use a sponge on a stick.

Neatening the rim
To give a crisp, clean finish to the rim of your pot use a strip of wet chamois leather pinched lightly around the rim as the wheel rotates, or alternatively you can use a strip of polythene. Strips cut from the bag the clay came in work perfectly for this.

181

Knuckling up variations

There are variations on the knuckling up method of forming a cylinder.

Method one: Use your fingertips on both the inside and outside to lift and shape the form.

Method two: Use the side of the forefinger of your right hand on the outside of the form and the fingers of your left hand on the inside.

Smooth off the outside of the cylinder by replacing the fingers of your right hand with either a wooden, metal or plastic rib. You can also lift the wall this way, with practice.

182

Stress-free lifting off

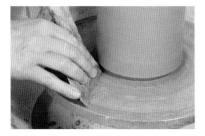

1 Remove all excess clay from the base of the pot using a rib held at an angle of 45 degrees to the pot and the wheel head. (This angle will ensure that the surplus clay travels up the back of the rib, away from the pot.) Now, with the rib still at 45 degrees, cut a bevel at the base of the pot to allow a clean transit of the wire.

2 Make sure the wheel head and wire are clean then, holding the wire taut, pass it under the base of the pot.

3 Make sure your hands are clean and dry, and then cup them around the pot as near to the base as possible. Gently tilt the pot back towards your body as you lift. This allows air to pass underneath and releases suction as the pot is lifted, and makes the procedure much easier. Transfer the pot to a board as quickly as possible.

Making lifting off easier

• As an aid to lifting, lay a sheet of uncreased newspaper over the rim of the pot; then, turning the wheel very slowly, run a finger over the rim to fix it in place. The resulting airtight seal will hold the shape as you lift, minimizing distortion.
• Use a hot-air gun or blowlamp to dry off the surface of the pot and firm up the clay a little before lifting it off the wheel head. This will help prevent distortion of the pot when lifting.
• Avoid touching up or correcting the shape of a pot once you have lifted it off the wheel head. Glaze will cover slight handprints but other corrections should be made at the leather-hard stage.

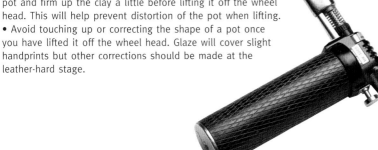

Before lifting your pot

Do:
• Remove excess water from the inside of the pot.
• Clean off the wheel around the base of the pot.
• Cut a bevel at the base.
• Ensure that your hands are clean and dry.
• Have a board close by, ready to put the pot on.

Don't:
• Flood the wheel head with water before lifting the pot – this will only saturate the clay at the base and can distort the form badly.
• Delay in lifting the pot once you have wired it through.

SEE ALSO:
Developing ideas,
34–35
Developing form,
36–37

Altering the basic cylinder

You can use cylinders as the starting point from which to create many other forms, but to be successful, the balance and proportion must be correct. From mugs and cups to pitchers, vases and jars, the principles of altering a form are all the same – follow the easy steps on these pages to learn all you need to know.

Making a bellied vase

1 Throw a basic cylinder, leaving an amount of clay on the top edge of the pot as a fat rim. This weight of clay is required to give a visually bold rim to a vase or to form the lip for a pitcher if you want to adapt the form further.

2 Using a rib on the outside as support and to keep the surface smooth, apply gentle pressure to push the clay out with your fingers from the inside, beginning from the base and stopping at the two-thirds point.

3 Remember to lubricate as necessary.

Mark a line

If it helps, draw a line in the cylinder with a rib to mark where the belly will end and the neck begin.

4 Throw the remaining neck third using the pinch and lift method (see page 91). To narrow the neck further, apply slightly more pressure from the outside when lifting and then finish the shape by slightly flaring the neck out at the rim. You now have a basic vase. You can also use this technique to make cups and mugs, or follow the steps on the next page to adapt the vessel into a pitcher.

Visualize the cylinder in thirds – the lower two thirds form the belly of the pot, and the upper third forms the neck.

184

Adapting the bellied vase to make a pitcher

1 Create the lip of the pitcher by thinning out a small section of the thickened edge of the pot between your finger and thumb. Lifting the clay from underneath, even it out neatly to the edge, taking care not to thin it too much or it will become ragged.

2 Gently squeeze the thinned lip around the forefinger of your right hand, using the thumb and finger of your left hand. Carefully roll your finger from side to side to give the lip a slight "throat", while still holding the clay surrounding it. Remove your fingers carefully to avoid distorting the shape. (For making and applying a handle, see pages 116–117.)

185

Forming a gallery for a lid

Throw a cylinder with a thick rim (as for the pitcher, above). You will need this weight at the top to form the gallery. Place the thumb of your left hand on the outside of the rim and the second finger of your left hand inside the rim, so that the forefinger can come down between them to spread the clay open for the gallery. The right hand is only used to steady the left hand as the clay is rotating.

Remember to relax your hands when you have finished making the gallery to allow the form to settle before removing them altogether. Measure the gallery at this stage to enable you make the lid to the right size. (See "Throwing off the hump" on page 109.)

This cross section shows the correct hand position when you are forming the gallery or recess for a lid.

Adapting a cylinder to make a bottle

1 Throw a cylinder, leaving some weight at the rim.

2 Place your left thumb over your right thumb. Both second fingers go around the outside of the pot. Position a forefinger inside the pot.

3 Using a gentle strangling action, bring your hands together, moving inwards and upwards at the same time. It is essential to get the balance of this right because the clay must have space to travel.

4 As you increase your grip, the diameter of the top will decrease and any unevenness will present itself as a ripple. (If appropriate, remove this with a pin or wire.)

Hand position for collaring in

Hand position is critical for the "collaring in" procedure (step 2). Here you can see the hands pulled away from the pot. Your left thumb should be placed over the right; second fingers are placed around the pot as if strangling it, and your right forefinger goes inside the pot.

5 Once you have achieved the narrowness required at the neck, shape and form the top of the pot as though it were a small pot on top of a big pot, following the procedures previously described. Remember to consolidate the rim with your finger, a strip of chamois or polythene.

Forming narrow spouts on bottle forms

You can make an assortment of necks using the basic collaring-in process (see the Decorative wares directory on pages 146–151 for inspiration), but the technique of creating a narrow neck or spout on a bulbous bottle form is one of the more complicated – think of it as throwing a small form on top of a larger one.

1 Collar the neck of the bottle in to the point where your finger will no longer fit inside.

2 Replace your finger with a tool such as a pencil, brush handle or chopstick, and continue to throw the neck upwards using your fingers on the outside.

188

Throwing a faceted bowl

1 Throw a cylinder approximately 2 cm (3/4 in) thick from base to top. (The thickness of the wall must be even throughout.) Flatten the top, then push in the base with the forefinger of your right hand to form a simple goblet shape. This is essential for cutting the facets because it gives the wire somewhere to start and finish.

2 Cut the facets from the wall of the cylinder with a wire held taut between your two hands. Cut on the far side of the cylinder, and from top to bottom. Turn the cylinder to make each cut on the opposite side from you, working around the form until you have made eight cuts.

3 You can achieve great height using this method, but make sure the height looks balanced in proportion to the body of the bottle.

Adding decoration
You can add a simple spiral decorative feature if you like by running the edge of a rib up the length of the neck while continuing to support the inside with the stick.

3 When you belly out the form, your hands must not touch the outside as this would destroy the facets cut by the wire. Use both hands to gently belly out the form from the inside, working from base to top. Repeat this as often as required to achieve a balanced shape.

4 To finish, gently run a rib over the rim while supporting the form from the inside with the other hand. This will flatten and splay the rim, giving a slightly ragged appearance that can be neatened up at the leather-hard stage if required.

TRY IT

 Give the sides texture

Using a twisted metal wire to cut facets will give the surface a textured finish.

SEE ALSO:

Clays,
10–13
Improvising tools,
26–27

Tips for decorating at the wet stage

Adding surface decoration at the wet stage and then continuing with the making process is a fantastic shortcut to many interesting and even sculptural effects.

An easy twisted texture

1 Throw a cylinder with a slightly narrower middle then, using a forked tool, scratch a pattern into the clay from top to base and at measured intervals around the pot.

2 Belly the pot out from the inside only, as for the faceted bowl on page 97, then finish off the rim with a rib. The pattern you create will twist as the form is bellied out. Repeat until you are happy with the shape.

Creating "volcanic" effects

This technique introduces dry clay to the surface of the wet cylinder prior to shaping the pot. You can use any dry clay – china clay, ball clay and so on – but do experiment with clays that fire to different temperatures, such as red earthenware on white stoneware or porcelain on red earthenware. The results can be very exciting.

1 Wet the surface of the pre-thrown cylinder with water or slurry. Cup the dry clay in your right hand and then gently apply it to the surface as the wheel rotates slowly.

2 Neaten up the rim of the pot, removing any dry clay from this area in the process. Clean the wheel head and cut a bevel at the base of the cylinder.

3 Belly out the form from the inside until you are happy with the shape. The resulting surface will look volcanic or rocklike; you can enhance it further by rubbing oxides into it before its final firing.

192
Creating texture and colour together

This is probably the only technique where you would apply slip in this way. Remember, you are not aiming for a perfectly coated surface – the slip is intended to add a textural quality and introduce another colour.

1 Throw a slightly thick cylinder and rib the outside wall to remove excess slurry and water. Pour some slip into your right hand.

2 Apply the slip to the wall of the cylinder as the wheel rotates slowly. Support the wall from inside with your other hand.

3 With the wheel rotating slowly and your fingers slightly splayed, gently move them up and down in a wavelike motion over the surface of the pot. Neaten and finish the rim and the base.

4 Belly the pot out from the inside only, until you are happy with the shape.

Drying for lift-off

Ideally, this type of pot would be thrown on a wooden bat because it cannot be lifted off the wheel head in its wet state. Dry the surface off with a blowtorch or heat gun until it is touch-dry. Make sure the wheel is rotating as you dry for evenness.

TRY IT

 Lifting the pot off with the help of a balloon

Wire-off the base then inflate a round balloon inside the pot to a size suitable to hold the weight. Quickly lift the pot off and onto a board, and allow the balloon to deflate. Be careful – the balloon can suck in the sides of the pot as you lift so you must work quickly. Always keep a few balloons handy in different sizes – this tip works for all kinds of pots.

194
Carving for sculptural effects

1 Throw a slightly thick cylinder and rib off the walls so they are straight, neat and free from slurry. Flatten the rim with a rib to create a "stop point" to carve to.

2 Using the pointed edge of a wooden or metal rib, gently carve the wall of the cylinder by moving the rib up and down in a wavelike action as the wheel rotates slowly. Begin at the base and work up to the rim, supporting the wall from the inside as you work.

3 Belly out the pot from the inside only, until you are happy with the shape; then cut and lift it off the wheel.

195

Six great decorative techniques

These techniques can all be used to decorate the cylinder wall in its straight form, prior to bellying out, or even afterwards as long as the form has not been faceted.

Soft squaring
This technique is especially suited to small items such as tea bowls or mugs. Begin by pulling your fingers up the inside of the cylinder to form a rough square shape, then repeat the action using a piece of wooden dowel or similar tool to square off the sides and rim.

Rouletting
Roll a patterned roulette wheel around the wall of the pot as it rotates slowly on the wheel. This type of decorating tool can be improvised from string wound around sticks, or small, thick cylinders made of clay, wood or plaster with impressed or carved patterns.

Fine grooves
Use a serrated kidney to make straight or wavy lines in the clay.

Experimental tools
Use string, cord, rope and textured rollers and cylinders that you find, buy or make yourself to produce a myriad of textured effects in the wet clay surface.

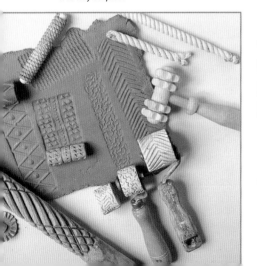

Ridges
Cut different-sized grooves into an old credit card to make a former. Support the pot from the inside as you make the ridges on the outside.

Horizontal grooves
Use the first finger of your right hand to score grooves around the pot at regular or irregular intervals. Support the wall from the inside as you do this.

196

Seven steps from round to oval

When making an oval dish from a basic cylinder, it is critical that the walls of the cylinder are truly vertical with no outward flare. It is actually preferable for the walls to have a slightly inward lean, because when the section is removed from the base and the walls are pushed together, the long sides of the dish will tend to flare outwards. If they are flared to begin with, at this stage they would simply flop straight over on their sides.

1 Throw a wide-based cylinder with a flattened rim to your required height. Clean off the wheel head, bevel the base edge, and wire under the base. Allow the pot to dry off a little.

2 Using a potter's knife, cut a leaf-shaped section out of the base, bearing in mind that the fatter the cut section, the narrower the dish will be. Lift this section out carefully.

3 With your hands cupped on both long sides of the dish, gently push them together until the edges from the cutaway section meet.

4 Blend the clay over the join – if you wish you can use a coil of soft clay pressed over the join to help reinforce it.

5 For a neat finish, use a damp sponge or rib to smooth over the clay in the base of the dish.

6 When the dish is firm enough to handle, turn it over onto a clean board. You may need to wire it off again before you can lift it. Reinforce the cut line with a coil of soft clay. Blend it in well but take care to avoid pushing the base in.

7 Finish by running a rib or kidney over the base for a smooth finish. Turn the dish the right way up and run a rib or kidney over the inside one more time to make sure the base dries flat.

Brilliant bowls

The principles of throwing bowls are slightly different to those for cylinders because the focus is on the interior shape and profile rather than the exterior, which is developed later. From centring the clay to developing the bowl shape, the following hints and tips will ensure success for any weight of clay.

 197

Basic bowl success

The key to throwing a successful bowl is to allow enough weight at the base to support the wall as it is thrown outwards and to form the foot ring later when the bowl is turned. These drawings show types of bowls in cross section. Each indicates how much clay is required at the base to successfully support the weight of the wall and also shows the turned foot ring.

A rounded foot ring gives an interesting twist to this bowl's profile.

Use a throwing rib to form a hollow, at the throwing stage, or at the same time that you turn the base.

A shallow bowl with a wide base may need an extra foot ring to support the centre during firing.

No handles are necessary for this elegant, straight-sided open cone shape.

1 Centre the clay to a doorknob shape. This allows your fingers underneath to lift the wall so that there is enough clay to support the wall without it being excessive.

3 Pinch and lift the wall of the bowl, working from the centre upwards and slightly outwards to create a funnel shape.

5 Using your fingers or a rib, gently press the wall of the clay on the inside to create the curve of the bowl. Warning: If this is done too soon the bowl will have a tendency to slump down on itself.

2 Open the centre of the clay up to the required depth, keeping the clay in the base rounded (unlike for the cylinder where it was flattened).

4 Establish the width of the top of the bowl as quickly as possible by gently easing the clay up using the knuckling up technique (see pages 92–93).

6 Neaten up the outside wall of the bowl with a rib and finish the rim. Clean the wheel head and finish the base of the bowl as for a basic cylinder (see page 93), before wiring off and lifting it onto a board.

How to get the shape you want

A wide, shallow bowl

The principles are the same as for the basic except that it is opened wider at the base before lifting the walls. The key to success is to leave enough clay at the base to support the flare of the bowl.

A bowl with a flattened rim

1 Centre, open up and lift the clay as for the first bowl, but leave an amount of clay at the edge as a fat rim.

2 Pinch and lift the fat rim at a slightly more flared angle to the bowl but keep it slightly concave. If it is opened too wide at this stage it will flop over.

3 When the rim is finished, curve out the belly of the bowl.

4 Neaten the bowl up carefully using a rib or kidney to give a smooth surface for decorating later. Remember to support the rim from underneath as you run the rib over the upper surface.

FIX IT

199 **Common problems:**

The wall has collapsed
- This could be because the base is too narrow to support the weight of the wall as you have lifted it outwards. Try again from a wider base.
- You may have over-thinned the walls at the midsection. This creates a weak point that cannot support the weight from above. Try to throw the walls evenly from base to rim.

The bowls warp or break at the rim
- The clay naturally thins as the diameter of a bowl is widened. Throw the wall evenly and stop just short of the edge so that there is a slightly fatter section of clay to form the rim.
- Remember to consolidate the clay at the rim with a strip of chamois or polythene when you have finished.
- If the problem is beyond repair, remove the thin section with a pin or wire and re-consolidate the rim.

SEE ALSO:

Opening up,
90–91

Perfect plates

Plates are always best thrown on wooden bats to prevent distortion from handling at the wet stage. So, unless you have a dedicated wheel head, throwing the perfect plate begins by learning how to attach a bat to the wheel head.

Attaching a bat

1 Throw a pad of soft clay to cover the wheel head that is 2–2.5 cm (1/2–1 in) thick. Use either the side of your finger or a rib to achieve a level surface.

2 Using your finger or a tool, press gullies into the clay at approximately 2.5 cm (1 in) intervals, from the centre to the outside edge.

3 Neither the clay nor the bat should be wet, because excessive water will cause the bat to slide. Clean off any dust on the bat then position it centrally on the clay pad. Thump the bat a few times to secure it onto the clay.

Easy bat removal

To remove a bat from the wheel head after throwing, push a potter's knife sideways between the bat and the wheel head then twist it until the bat releases.

The clay pad can be used as long as it remains soft enough.

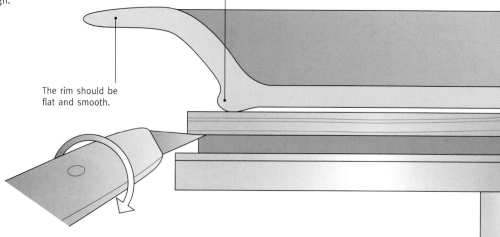

The roll foot acts as a point to glaze to when decorating the plate.

The rim should be flat and smooth.

201

Throwing a plate that won't collapse

1 As for a basic cylinder, centre your clay and open it out to create the base. This must be thick enough to later turn a foot ring – around 5–8 mm (1/4–1/2 in) thick for a dinner plate. Leave a weight of clay at the edge to form the rim of the plate. This weight, together with that of the base, will determine the final diameter of the plate.

2 Compress the clay in the base of the plate to prevent cracking, and consolidate the rim to keep it running true. Supporting the edge with your right hand on the outside and your finger and thumb in the pinch and lift position, squeeze the clay and gently pull it up to begin with.

3 As the clay of the rim thins, gently ease it outwards. It is very important to ensure that the face of the rim is slightly concave and the underside is convex to prevent the rim from collapsing due to gravity.

4 Use ribs and kidneys to refine the surface of the plate and reconsolidate the clay in the base.

5 Only refine the rim at the very end of the throwing process, especially if the clay is very soft. Don't overwork it because excessive rotation of the wheel will cause the rim to collapse.

6 Add decorative details such as lines and swirls if required, before turning the underside in preparation for wiring under the base. Lift the bat from the wheel head but do not handle the plate until it has stiffened to leather-hardness.

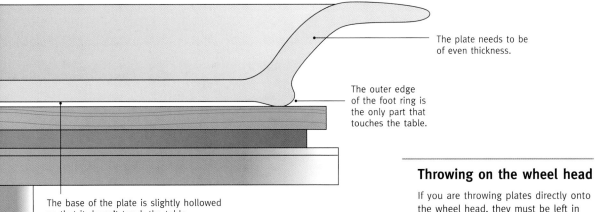

The plate needs to be of even thickness.

The outer edge of the foot ring is the only part that touches the table.

The base of the plate is slightly hollowed so that it doesn't touch the table.

Throwing on the wheel head

If you are throwing plates directly onto the wheel head, they must be left in place to stiffen up before removing.

Throwing in sections

It is very difficult to centre the amount of clay required to make large pots, so they are usually made in sections that are joined together to build up the size gradually. It is essential to use bats when working in this way.

SEE ALSO:
Coiling,
72–73

Making a pot bigger with coils

One way to increase the height of a pot is to add on, then throw, thick coils. You can also use this technique to make thicker or decorative rims. Form a ball of clay into a ring doughnut shape by pressing your finger or thumb through the centre then gradually shaping the ring to fit the opening on your pot. The advantage of making the coil in this way is that there will be no join in the coil when fitted onto the rim, which makes it easier to throw on.

1 Join the ring onto the top of the cylinder then use your fingers to blend the two surfaces together.

2 Apply a small amount of water, then centre the clay carefully between the finger and thumb of your left hand, using your other hand for support.

3 Throw the added coil as you like; to make the pot taller, to add a rim, or whatever.

Keeping the rim soft
Before adding the coil to the rim of your pot you must check that in terms of stiffness, the pot is strong enough to hold the weight of extra clay. However, the rim itself should be soft enough to match the clay that is to be added on. To overcome this potential problem, cover the rim with polythene to keep it soft while the rest of the form stiffens off to a manageable state.

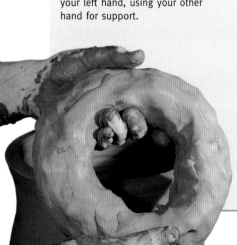

FIX IT

 Why use coils to increase the size?

• Adding coils allows you to increase the size of a pot in manageable stages.
• It is easier to introduce subtle changes in shape if you are only dealing with a small amount of clay at a time.
• Any number of coils can be added to increase height.
• The adding coils technique is the best method of adding extra clay to form decorative rims on large pots.

Planning your work

The clay walls of pots thrown in sections must be thick enough to support the weight of each additional section.

If you think the clay is too soft to continue to throw the form after adding a section, leave it to stiffen off before continuing. Alternatively, speed up the process by using a gas torch or hot-air gun to stiffen the clay. Do this as it rotates slowly on the wheel for even drying.

It is a good idea to work on several larger pots at the same time. Allowing sections to firm up while you work on the next means you can come back to them at the optimum moment to continue. Any number of sections can be added in this way providing the clay is firm enough to hold each addition and, as you improve, you will be able to join sections of different shapes.

Some forms are easier to join in sections rather than throw in one piece, like those with crisp changes of angle (see diagram below).

The upper section of a large pot is situated on the base section while both are still in place on their respective bats.

Oval pot with fluted upper section

Tapered upper section

Squat pot with flared upper section

How to throw a tall pot in two sections

1 Throw the top section first: a wide cylinder. You can open the clay completely at the base because this will be the top of the pot. Measure the diameter of the pot using calipers, then remove it from the wheel head but leave it on the bat.

2 Throw the lower section with a base to approximately the same size as the first cylinder then, following the principles described on page 95, make a gallery in the upper edge to exactly the same diameter as the opening of the first cylinder.

3 Accurate measurement is essential, because as soon as the sections come together as soft clay it is almost impossible to separate them.

4 Turn the first cylinder upside down while it is still in position on the bat, then gently position it inside the gallery of the second cylinder.

5 Carefully throw the two cylinders together by compressing the clay on the outside with your fingers. The bat should still be in place on top for this and the wheel should not be rotating too quickly.

6 Cut the bat from the top of the pot then consolidate the clay on the inside using your fingers and outside using a rib to make sure the join is secure. You can now carefully belly or refine the shape to your own design following the same principles as for a basic cylinder (see pages 94–97).

Tips for decorating rims at the wet stage

Here are some ideas for adding decorative rim details and features while the clay is still wet.

206 Keeping the pot light

Hollow rims are useful when you want to add visual balance or specific details to the top of a pot without increasing the weight too much. They can be thrown from added-on coils (see page 106) or made from cylinder forms with an excess of height.

An idea for an easy decorative rim

Holding your finger at a slight angle, press it into the clay at regular intervals around a flared rim to create a pie crust effect. Support the rim from the inside of the pot as you do this.

1 Once you have thrown your cylinder, gently ease the rim over using a curved rib. Work slowly and carefully, because excessive speed will cause the clay to flop over rather than curve.

2 Containing the rim carefully between the fingers and thumb of your left hand, continue to encourage the clay over with your right hand until it meets the outer wall of the cylinder.

3 Now gently join the two surfaces together until they are sealed, then neaten up the wall of the cylinder with a rib to remove excess clay or slurry.

4 If you want to add extra detail, try applying a decorative finish to the rim by combing it with a serrated tool.

FIX IT

207 Pots exploding?

You must release the air contained in a hollow rim before firing, otherwise it may explode. Do this by piercing the rim with a pin in a discreet place when the pot is still leather-hard.

Throwing lids

The term "throwing off the hump" is used to describe the practice of throwing a series of pots from one large lump of clay. It's ideal for making small items such as lids.

Cross section of a lid sitting on a pot.

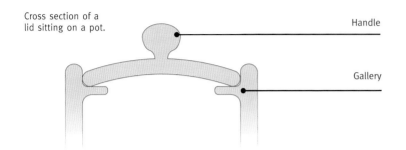

Handle

Gallery

Throwing off the hump

1 Centre a larger-than-necessary ball of clay – this is usually referred to as the "hump" – then create a small doorknob shape at the top of the clay.

2 Press the thumb of your right hand into the centre of the clay to form a small doughnut shape.

3 Open out and lift the shape by knuckling up (see pages 92–93) to create a miniature bowl form. Flatten off the rim a little between your fingers and thumb, or use a rib. This will keep the lid from warping and gives it an edge to sit on inside the pot.

4 Sponge out the inside of the lid then, using a pin or the point of a rib, score a line around the inside of the lid close to the rim, as a marker for waxing and glazing later.

Hand position for opening out
Here you can see the correct hand position for opening up and shaping the miniature bowl form (step 2).

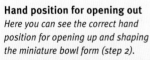

5 Using a rib, trim away excess weight from the underside of the lid. Then, using the point of the rib, cut a "v" just underneath to mark where the lid will be wired off.

6 Wire underneath the lid and then lift it off carefully onto a board. Dry the lid to leather-hardness before trimming.

209 A perfect fit

Using a pair of calipers, set one tip against the rim's inside edge (at the widest point in the opening) and the second tip just wider than the inside edge of the gallery (the narrowest point in the opening). This will give just enough play for a comfortable fit. Set the calipers aside at this width so you can measure the lid once you have made it and achieve the perfect fit. Remember to measure the lid regularly as you make it to ensure it is the right size.

The corresponding measurement for this type of lid is made on the inside of the rim of the pot.

The measurement for this lid is taken outside of the gallery because this is the part of the lid that will sit on the rim of the pot.

210 Throwing a lid with a gallery

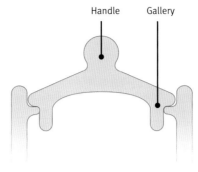

Handle   Gallery

Cross section of a flanged lid sitting on a pot.

1 Throw a small bowl shape off the hump (as for the lid on page 109), but leave some extra weight at the rim.

2 Split the rim using the second finger of your right hand, or a tool, while supporting the inside with the fingers of your left hand. This will create a "gallery" to sit inside the pot (as opposed to the whole lid sitting inside the pot).

3 Neaten the underside of the lid and cut a "v" shape. Then wire off and move the lid onto a board to firm up, ready for turning later.

FIX IT

211 Lids not fitting?

Accurate measuring is the most important part of making a lidded pot successfully. The lid should be neither too tight nor too loose so your measurement should allow a slight tolerance for this. Always use a pair of calipers to help you get the measurements right.

Making a lid with a knob

A lid with a knob for lifting is made to completion at the throwing stage, with the knob already in place. The one shown here is of the type that sits inside and on the gallery of the pot.

1 Centre a small doorknob of clay as for the previous two lids but instead of opening out from the centre, open the clay to one side of the centre. This will automatically create a knob shape in the centre of the ball.

2 Refine the shape of the knob first: Using the finger and thumb of your left hand and the second finger of your right hand, you can make it as ornamental as you choose.

3 Now open up the weight of clay around the knob to form a bowl shape, then flatten the rim to form the edge of the lid, which will sit on the gallery inside the pot.

Finish the underside of the lid in the same way as for the previous two lids, then wire off and transfer to a board.

Lid tips

• Always prepare the clay for a lid from the same batch as the container so that the shrinkage rate is exactly the same.
• Throw the container and lid together if possible – the container first and the lid second.
• Make regular, accurate measurements to obtain the correct fit.

This type of lid is measured at its widest point because the whole thing will fit on a gallery inside the pot. Measure the opening of the pot for this type of lid so that the calipers sit on the gallery.

The finished lid in position, resting on the gallery.

SEE ALSO:

Altering the basic
cylinder,
94–97

Super spouts

Spouts are generally thrown from a relatively small amount of
clay – 225 g (1/2 lb) or less – but they should always be
made longer than necessary to allow for the shape to be cut
to the correct size for your pot later. Always throw a couple of
spares in case you make a mistake with the first one.

Adapting spouts for other uses

Spouts do not always have to be made
for tea or coffee pots. You can adapt
the technique to make thrown necks to
fit on pots made by other methods, or
to make handles for other thrown forms.

Here, a thrown spout has been cut to fit
a slabbed bottle form. When joining
spouts to other forms in this way you
must score and slip both surfaces prior
to fitting them together.

FIX IT

214   **Spouts breaking?**

• It is absolutely essential that the
clay is in perfect condition for
throwing spouts – neither too soft
nor too hard – as great strain is put
on the clay when you narrow it off
to form the spout.
• Throw spouts as smoothly as
possible – excessive twisting will
cause warping when the pot is fired,
especially in high-fired varieties such
as stoneware and porcelain.

213

Throwing a great spout

1 Centre and pull up the clay as
for a basic cylinder, and then follow
the procedure for collaring in (see
page 96).

2 To keep the spout narrow, use the
first finger of your left hand inside and
your thumb on the outside, while also
using the fingers of your right hand to
lift the wall to the required height.

If you want a spout that is narrower
than your finger, use a pencil, brush
handle or chopstick to support the
inside while you refine the shape.

Spout variations

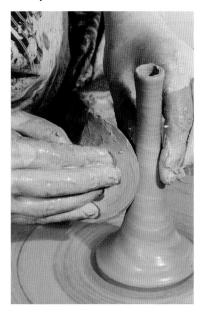

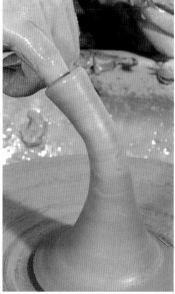

Longer spouts

Most spouts start as a simple, upside-down funnel shape – it is the elongating, bending, cutting, fitting or faceting of this simple form that creates variation. Longer spouts, for coffee pots for example, are slightly more complicated because of the extra length. Extra height is needed for trimming to the correct shape later. It is essential to use a tool on the inside for stability as you throw.

Curved spouts

Curved spouts will benefit from having a slight bend put into the top while they are still on the wheel head. This is done while the clay is still soft simply by inserting a finger.

Fitting the spout to another form

Pack the form with scrunched newspaper before fitting the spout to keep the walls from distorting as you work. The newspaper will burn away when the pot is biscuit-fired.

This example shows a thrown spout fitted to a mould-made vessel.

Long spouts should be left a while for the clay to stiffen before carefully bending into an "s" shape.

Faceted spouts

Faceted spouts are generally thrown straight with a thicker wall to allow for the shape to be cut later. The facets can be cut with a wire while the spout is still on the wheel, or at the leather-hard stage.

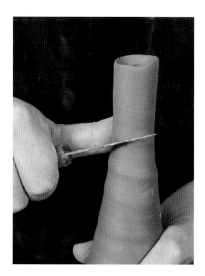

If you find the balance of the vessel is not quite right you can make refinements to height or angle of the rim once the spout is fitted onto it.

SEE ALSO:

Super spouts,
112–113
Altering the basic
cylinder,
94–97

Six perfect spouts

The most important quality of a spout is that it pours well without dripping or dribbling, but for both functional and aesthetic reasons it is also important that the spout is proportionally balanced with other components of the pot. If you follow the fundamental rules set out here, you will always be able to make the correct spout for your chosen pot.

Traditional spout

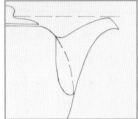

This spout is short and rounded; it is typical of the sort thrown by studio potters and should be fitted to a teapot with a rounded body.

The spout is attached to the upper swell of the pot to be in line with the highest point of the form.

Throw the spout following the basic instructions on pages 112–113. After wiring the spout off the wheel head, while the clay is still soft enough to manipulate, insert a little finger in the narrow end and gently bend the spout over a little to give a slight curve. When leather-hard, cut the spout to fit the shape of the pot, leaving it rounded at the point where it fixes onto the pot.

For pear shapes

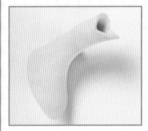
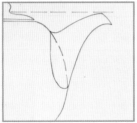

This slightly longer spout is ideally suited to a pear-shaped pot; it should be positioned just above the widest part of the pot but lower than the previous example. It is a general rule that longer spouts should be fixed lower down the pot but the open end of the spout should be higher than the highest liquid level in the pot.

The end of the spout has been cut in the style of silverware. Vaguely resembling a bird's beak, this feature adds character to the spout.

The base of the spout is cut to an oval shape to be in keeping with the shape of the pot.

For wider bottoms

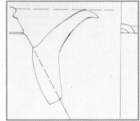

This spout is perfect for a straight-sided pot that looks triangular in profile or is wider at the base than the top.

Throw this one a little longer than usual to allow enough clay to be cut away to get the angle correct when positioning on the pot. It is best positioned halfway up the side of the pot.

Cut the tip of the spout at a slight angle and square the base off to be in line with the bottom of the pot.

For squats

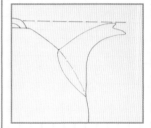

Perfect for a pot that is rounded and squat but wider at the base than the top; this spout is shorter than the previous example, but you will still need enough length to be able to cut it to the right size. Curve the spout over a little at the soft stage then cut the tip in the silverware style at leather-hard. This gives a good taper and flare for pouring.

The base of the spout is cut to a point and is shield-like in shape.

Multi-faceted

Long and elegant

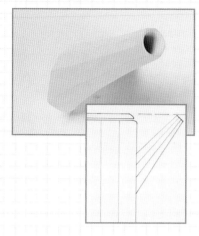

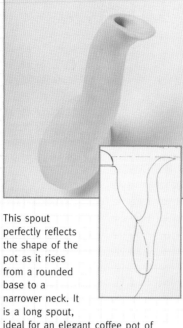

Ideally suited to a contemporary coffee pot, this spout is best fitted to a tall cylindrical body that has been faceted in from base to top.

Throw the spout thickly to allow for faceting at the leather-hard stage and make it as long as possible. Keep the sides straight as you collar the shape in and ensure an even thickness to the clay wall.

Use a knife, cutting wire or metal kidney to cut the facets, cutting from the tip down to the base.

This spout perfectly reflects the shape of the pot as it rises from a rounded base to a narrower neck. It is a long spout, ideal for an elegant coffee pot of traditional proportions.

The spout should be positioned quite low down on the widest part of the pot so that the top is in line or just above the highest point of the pot when the lid is in place (see above).

Manipulate the shape of the spout with a small finger after wiring off the wheel head. First angle the spout back a little in one direction then angle the tip forwards again.

Cut the rest to shape at the leather-hard stage, leaving the base rounded to match the shape of the pot.

217

The planning stages

Before starting to throw, jot down your design ideas, paying particular attention to where the components will be positioned.

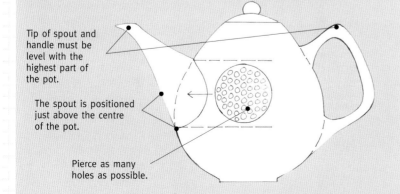

Tip of spout and handle must be level with the highest part of the pot.

The spout is positioned just above the centre of the pot.

Pierce as many holes as possible.

SEE ALSO:
Coiling,
72–73
Slabbing,
40–41

Handles and knobs

Handles for pots can be made in many different ways to add style and an individual statement to your work. The following techniques will give you some inspirational ideas to use as a starting point for experimentation.

Two methods for handles

Handles can be made in two ways. In the first method, "pulling on the pot", the clay is joined to the pot then pulled into shape. The second method, "pulling off the pot", involves making the handle separately, then joining it to the pot.

Pulling on the pot

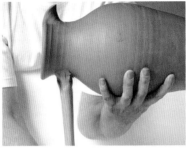 

1 Attach a fat coil of clay to the body of your pot at the correct position for the top of the handle. With a well lubricated hand, pull the clay gently but firmly downwards between your fingers and thumb.

2 Curve the handle into shape and attach the base of the handle securely to the base of the pot.

Pulling off the pot

1 Form a fat coil of clay then, holding it in one hand, draw the clay down between your fingers and thumb. You can make the coil oval or round depending on how you shape your hand. Keep your hand lubricated for this process.

2 Pull the handle longer than you need to give some play for attaching to the pot, or to make several handles at a time. Place the handle flat on the edge of a table or board to stiffen up before fitting it onto the pot.

3 Attach the upper end of the handle firmly to the leather-hard pot, having first marked and then scored and slipped the area. Bend and shape the handle to suit the profile of the pot, and fix the lower end in place.

220   Press a decorative detail

Press a stamp into the soft clay at the base of a handle to add a decorative detail. Some potters stamp their name or mark at this point.

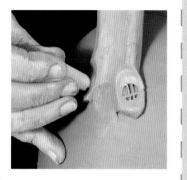

Coil handles

Textured coils can introduce lovely decorative details to simple forms. Try rolling the coils over textured surfaces such as old lace, vinyl wallpaper or rubber mats for rich patterns. Twist the coils into shape before fitting them onto your pot.

Slab handles

You can cut handles of many different profiles from slabs of clay. They can also be textured by rolling the clay between two sheets of texturing material. Take care to reinforce well when joining slab handles.

221   Throwing a knob onto a turned lid

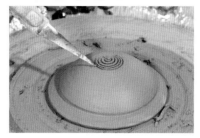

1 When your lid has been turned to the required shape (see pages 110–111), score an area on the top to form a "key" for the knob.

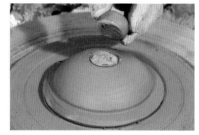

2 Roll a small ball of soft clay and flatten it on one side. Apply some slip to the scored area on the lid, then fix the ball in place.

3 Throw the knob between the fingers and thumbs of both hands to form the upright shape.

4 Use your little finger to underscore the knob and shape it further as required. Allow the lid to dry to leather-hardness, then trim to shape if required.

222   Lugs

Lug handles are attached to the sides of larger vessels and casserole dishes so that they can be lifted more easily. They can be made from thrown, coiled, pulled or extruded clay.

Thrown lug

Make the lug from a short, open cylinder, thrown slightly thicker at the base.

When it is leather-hard, cut a "v" section from each side of the cylinder, then join the sections onto the pot. Reinforce the joins with coils of clay.

Lugs made by other methods

Make this handle by either pulling, coiling or extruding the clay, and fix onto the side in the same way as for the thrown lug. You can stamp the clay at the ends of the lugs for decorative detail if you like – see the box on this page, top left.

SEE ALSO:
Preparing clay,
  18
Coiling,
  72–73

Six ideas for handles and knobs

A lid can be transformed from a simple utilitarian object to a work of art by adding a quirky handle or knob. Here are six examples of the same lid with different finishes to give you a starting point for your own experimentation.

Coiled handle

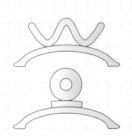

A better finish can be achieved by adding smaller coils to each end of a handle to conceal the points where it has been joined onto the lid. Try some of these other ideas for making coiled handles or experiment with ideas of your own.

Birds

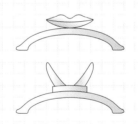

You can have great fun modelling simple little birds as handles for lids. Animals or fish also work very well. Try modelling something outrageous or unusual that will create a conversation piece!

Slabbed

Try cutting unusual shaped sections from slabs, then piercing them with a hole-cutter as an extra feature. Fixing the handle onto a small, flattened ball of clay before fitting onto the lid will also add extra detail. The possibilities for these are endless – just play with different shapes until you find one you like – doodling on paper is a good way to create ideas for these.

FIX IT

223 Measuring and fixing the handle

• Make sure the size of the handle is in proportion to the size of the lid – try making the handle in card first to get the measurement right. Alternately, make a quick clay maquette – size and proportion is much easier measured this way.

• The handle must be at the same stage of hardness as the lid when joining the two together otherwise the parts will separate because the two components are drying at different speeds. Both parts should be leather-hard for easiest joining.

Leaf

Biscuit-cutters are great for cutting unusual shapes from slabs. This little leaf shape has been fixed onto a small ball of clay before being fixed to the lid. Cutters of this type are available in many shapes and sizes giving fantastic scope for experimentation. Scale these leaves up or down to use as templates for your lids. They can be attached at jaunty angles for added effect.

Butterflies

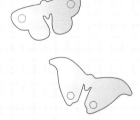

These little butterflies have again been made from slabs using biscuit-cutters, but here two have been joined at the centre and the wings splayed to give them more purchase on the handle. Butterflies and moths make very delicate decorations for the sides of boxes and jars – and on lids too.

Plaited

Try plaiting thin coils of clay to form a handle. Once they are fixed in place, you can impress a decorative stamp at each end or use this space to make your personal mark. The clay will need to be quite soft to plait successfully, but leave it to firm up before fitting it onto the lid. Once you have mastered the technique of plaiting clay, try some of these more complicated ideas – they are achievable with practice.

Turning

Turning is the term used for the process of trimming away excess clay from the base of thrown forms. Pots are usually turned at the leather-hard stage because they are easier to handle without risk of damage, and the clay will cut most precisely.

SEE ALSO:

Attaching a bat, 104
Brilliant bowls, 102–103

Turning tools

Potters often make their own tools for turning. Try, for example, making some from the metal strip used around the edges of packing cases. Alternately, your pottery supplier will have a good selection of bamboo and metal tools for turning.

Foot rings

The main reason for turning is to cut foot rings into the base of pots. A foot ring helps to define the shape of a pot and give it a visual lift. Turning is also used to narrow the base of pots to give a form the correct balance.

Knocking onto centre: the technique

"Knocking onto centre" is the term used for centring pots directly onto the wheel head for turning. It's a traditional method, but difficult to master. You'll need plenty of practise to accomplish this technique, but it is by far the best and fastest method if you have a lot of pots to turn.

Dampen the wheel head, then position your pot using the concentric lines to centre it as far as is possible. With the wheel rotating, look at the edge of the pot on the left side then, when you see a wobble, strike the opposite side of the pot with your other hand. Repeat the process until the pot runs true to centre.

TRY IT

225 Practise knocking onto centre

Practise knocking onto centre using different-sized vessels from your kitchen. Try bowls, cups, vases and so on. It will help you to learn the technique using different weights and shapes and save you having to throw vessels just to practise this technique.

Basic foot ring shapes

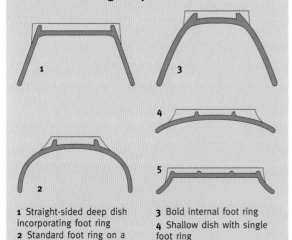

1 Straight-sided deep dish incorporating foot ring
2 Standard foot ring on a rounded pot
3 Bold internal foot ring
4 Shallow dish with single foot ring
5 Flat, wide plate with two foot rings

A simple way to fasten the form

Forming a pad is a simple way to fasten a form to the wheel head for turning. Do it at the end of a throwing session.

1 Throw a flat disc of clay and allow it to dry to leather-hard.

2 Trim the disc to form a pad with gullies, rings or lines to register the pots on centre.

226 The right time to turn

If a lid is to have a thrown knob attached to it, then choosing the correct time to turn is critical. The clay of the lid should not be too soft because this will make it vulnerable to collapse, but neither should it be too hard, because this will cause problems when you try to join it to softer clay. Somewhere just short of leather-hard is optimum but you will need to experiment for best results.

1 If the clay in your lid is soft, you can form a slight hump in the centre of the pad of clay to support the underside as you turn and then throw on the knob or apply a handle.

2 Centre the lid on the pad of clay. Using a turning tool, create the edge of the lid first, then turn away the excess weight of clay to form a dome.

Keeping a steady hand

Many people struggle to hold their hands steady when turning pots. Try positioning a piece of sturdy timber across the pan to lean on as you work. This is referred to as a "turning stick".

227 How to turn a bowl

1 Position your bowl in the precut gully in the pad of clay (see "A simple way to fasten the form", bottom right, opposite). You can dampen the rim slightly to make it stick if you need to.

2 The first cut in the turning process is made to check that the outer diameter of the pot is running true and the base is flat. Once you have done this, mark where the foot ring is going to be using the tip of your turning tool, then trim away the excess clay on the outside edge to the marked line.

3 Working within the marked line of the foot ring, trim away the excess clay from centre to edge, following the curve of the bowl. The cut will be deeper at the edge of the ring than in the centre. (The diagrams show the correct profile.)

4 Once you have trimmed the foot ring to the correct shape and size, cut a little mitre on the inner and outer edges to finish off. (The diagram shows this.)

TRY IT

228 Perfecting your trimming technique

• If the base of your pot has been cut with a twisted wire to create a pattern but you need to turn away the outside edge to refine the shape, place a plastic lid centrally over the base. You can safely rest your hand on the lid to trim the outside edge without spoiling the base, and use the lid as a marker to trim to.

• After trimming, the thickness of the clay wall should be even throughout the pot. Use a double caliper (see diagram) to measure the thickness when trimming.

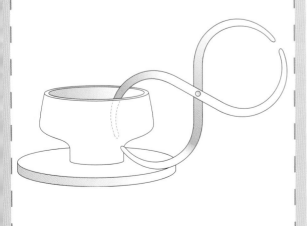

SEE ALSO:

Opening up,
   90–91
Knuckling up
and lifting off,
   92–93

Chucks and chums

Essentially chucks and chums are the same thing – devices for keeping pots on centre to trim. A chum is used to support a bowl or similar item from the inside and a chuck contains a form such as a bottle, which obviously cannot stand on its neck.

229

Making a chum

1 To make a chum for trimming bowls, throw a thick, open-based cylinder with a fat rim on a bat. The size of the chum will be dictated by the size of your bowl – it should sit comfortably on the rim.

2 Leave the chum in place on the bat and allow it to dry leather-hard before positioning the bowl over it to turn. You may need to make slight adjustments to the bowl to centre it exactly, but keeping the chum on the bat means that it is always perfectly centred.

Chucks are thrown in exactly the same way as chums but are taller and narrower to accommodate bottle-type forms. The pot is located inside the chuck to allow the base to be trimmed.

230

Making custom chucks and chums

You will need

- Wooden bats
- A selection of different-sized flowerpots
- Blocks of wood – small enough to fit into the base of the flowerpots
- Screws or bolts

Chucks and chums can be biscuit-fired for greater durability, but this creates the problem of centring each time they are used – try this great idea for making versions that don't need centring and will last a lifetime.

Drill a countersunk hole through the exact centre of a bat, then position the flowerpot over the hole. Position a block of wood inside the pot then screw all the sections together with a bolt. Use this method to make chucks of any size that are always centred and ready to use.

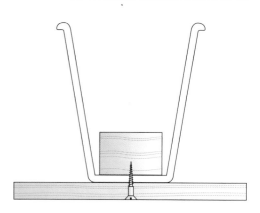

Decorative techniques at the green stage

The following decorative treatments are most suitable for pots that have firmed up a little but still have some flexibility to allow the clay to be manipulated.

Shaping techniques

Indenting

The clay must be stiff enough to handle without spoiling the surface decoration for this technique, but soft enough not to crack when you are manipulating it. Beginning on one side and working around the pot evenly, make a series of indentations with the fingers of one hand while supporting the wall from inside with your other hand. Now move down to the level below and make the next indentations between the first ones. Work down to the base in levels like this until the whole surface is indented.

Leather-hard squaring

1 Square off the sides of a trimmed vessel by gently tapping it on the worktop while applying hand pressure from either side.

2 Tap the walls with a wooden paddle to define the edges and square off more precisely.

Faceting

Pots can be faceted at the leather-hard stage as well as the soft stage. You will need to throw the pot with a thicker wall for this technique. Try using a potato peeler to shave away the clay – beginning at the base and working upwards. Cut grooves into the surface of the trimmed vessel using a sharp triangular tool. Cut them successively or at intervals down the pot. This gives a very precise, almost machine-turned finish.

Fluting

Use a loop tool to cut vertical grooves into the sides of a cylinder. It helps to mark the sections on the pot before you begin for equal spacing. Throw a slightly thicker-walled vessel for this technique. (You can also flute the surface horizontally by centring it on the wheel first.)

The striped glaze effect on this horizontally fluted vase works sympathetically with this decorative technique. The glaze is just beginning to break over the raised edges of the fluting, further accentuating the stripes.

232 Decorating with slip

In simple terms, "slip" is liquid clay. It can be coloured with stains and oxides to create bold or subtle shades and, although it is a very traditional medium for decorating pots, it has so many methods of application that it still offers versatility for personal expression.

Pouring

Pour slip from a pitcher to coat the whole surface of the pot, or just selected areas. Pour away excess quickly to prevent saturation.

Dipping

This method is particularly useful for forms that can be held inside. The pot should be on the dry side of leather-hard for dipping, and this should be accomplished as quickly as possible to avoid saturation. Allow the slip to drain from the bottom before wiping the excess away.

Brushing

Load a brush with slip and brush over the surface in even strokes. Allow it to dry a little before repeating the process for an even coating.

Slip can also be brushed on in a calligraphic way to create patterns using a soft, well-loaded brush.

Work in a free, painterly way to create dramatic, bold brush marks.

Sponging

Sponge slip over a clay surface as an alternative to brushing; you will need to build the layers up gradually for even coverage. Allow each coat to dry off a little before applying the next.

Use an open-textured, natural sponge to apply a light coat of slip in an alternate shade so that the colour below can show through.

Printing with sponges

You can use precut sponges and slip to print onto the surface of your pots. The slip needs to be fairly thick, but blot it onto paper after dipping to remove excess. You can build up colours and patterns very quickly using this method.

TRY IT

233 Cutting sponges

• Cut decorative designs into sponges easily by dampening and freezing the sponge first. You will find a craft knife cuts through the sponge easily this way to create even very intricate shapes.

• Alternately, use a hot wire to burn detail into a sponge. The wire can be manipulated into curves and shapes that would otherwise be hard to cut. However, burning sponge can be highly toxic so either work outside or make sure you have a good extraction system and wear a mask. Hot needles or soldering irons can be used for straight lines but the same precautions must be taken.

Combing

Make fluid marks by combing through slip with a wide-toothed comb. This works very well if a light slip is applied over a dark clay body or vice versa. Allow the slip to dry off slightly before combing. Alternately, use your fingers instead of a comb for a freer finish. Draw your fingers through the slip while it is still wet for the best results.

Using resist

The resist method uses paper shapes to create a design on the surface of a pot (similar to stencilling). The paper acts as a resist when slip is applied over the surface, leaving the design in sharp outline when the paper is removed. Newspaper is perfect for this technique.

1 Dampen your paper shapes in water before placing them onto a leather-hard surface. Make sure they are sealed down. If they are not, brush some water over them until they are flat.

2 Carefully sponge slip over the entire surface of the pot, including the paper shapes. If you want to add another colour, use an open-textured sponge to lightly cover the surface so you can still see the colour beneath. The first coating should be touch-dry before you do this. Remove the paper shapes carefully with a pin when the slip has dried to the touch.

TRY IT

 Combing tools

Raid the kitchen drawers for interesting gadgets to use for combing – tools for holding onions when slicing are particularly good. You can make your own combs from plastic credit cards – cut various sizes of teeth for different effects.

This pitcher by Willi Singleton has been decorated using the combed slip technique, then covered with transparent ash glaze. The decoration suits this simple but pleasing elongated form perfectly.

Paper shapes

If you leave a small area of the paper shapes exposed when applying slip you will be able to see them better when it is time to remove them.

Slip trailing

Slip trailing requires a bold and confident hand to achieve good results, but once mastered it becomes as deft a decorating process as using a brush or pencil. You will need a "slip-trailing bulb" for this technique. These are readily available in different sizes from pottery suppliers, but there are some alternatives you could try (see Tips, right).

Load the bulb with fairly thick slip then squeeze evenly and steadily to produce a continuous flow over a leather-hard surface. For continuous lines, place your work on a banding wheel and rotate as you apply the slip. You can mark the design out in pencil before you begin if it helps. Use the technique to make dots of various sizes as well as lines.

Slip trailing tips

- Slip trailing is a difficult technique to master, so practise on sheets of paper before you try it on clay.
- The bottles used in home-perm or hair-dye kits make good slip trailers, so try these as an alternative to practise with.

The outline of the simple design on this lovely country-style pitcher by Niek Hoogland was slip trailed to provide a framework for coloured glaze application.

Feathering

Feathering incorporates slip trailing onto a wet slip surface that is then dragged with a feather or pin to create a pattern. Flat, open forms are most suitable for this technique.

Coat the surface of your pot with slip using the pouring method (see page 124), then trail evenly spaced lines in a contrasting colour over the slip. The trailed colour should appear to "melt" into the slip.

Wax resist

Either hot wax or wax emulsion can be painted onto the surface of leather-hard clay before applying slip using one of the methods already described. This method is difficult for delicate detail and is more suited to free brushwork.

Marbling

This technique is most suited to flatter, more open forms – such as bowls and plates – because the slip has to be fluid to work well and therefore would simply not stay put on a steep-sided form.

Pour or trail areas of contrasting slip into an open form. Shake the form to move the colours around, but do not overdo it or they will become muddy and indistinguishable.

Sgraffito

Sgraffito is a form of incising or drawing into clay. The technique is often used on surfaces with a contrasting slip to the clay body so that when the design is drawn the clay colour is revealed. You can use any pointed tool for sgraffito – even a pencil – and the technique is suitable for all forms.

236

Even more ideas

Burnishing

Burnishing, or polishing, the surface of a pot compacts the clay particles to create a shiny surface. It is a technique most suited for low-fire treatments such as smoke firing or Raku where the clay body needs to be porous to absorb and retain the marks of the flame. The optimum time to burnish is at the leather-hard stage.

You can burnish the clay surface directly, but apply slip for a finer finish. Use polished pebbles or spoons and work over the surface in circular movements to avoid making marks. Repeat the process until the surface is shiny, then finish off by polishing with cotton wool or a piece of soft plastic stretched over your finger.

Inlay

Inlay is the technique of embedding contrasting coloured clays or slip into the surface of a pot. Any shaped pot is generally suitable for this type of decoration.

Incise or sgraffito your design into a leather-hard surface and then paint a contrasting coloured slip into the lines as thickly as possible. When the inlay has dried to the leather-hard stage, carefully scrape the excess slip away with a kidney to reveal the pattern underneath.

Incising or cutout work

The technique of incising involves cutting through the clay completely to create cut away patterns. This can be done using sharp knives or hole cutters.

Draw your design onto the surface of a leather-hard pot before cutting out the sections with a craft knife or hole-cutter. Carefully remove the cutaway clay, then gently wipe around the cut edges with a slightly damp sponge to soften them a little.

237

Burnishing

- Do not fire burnished ware above 1000°C (1832°F); 960°C (1760°F) is an optimum temperature to retain the shine.
- Do not handle the pot on the burnished surface – fingerprints are easily transferred and do not fire out.
- Use soft cotton gloves to handle the pot while burnishing and packing into the kiln for biscuit firing.

These porcelain slip-cast forms by Sue Dyer have been sensitively yet minimally inlaid to accentuate the form of the vessels.

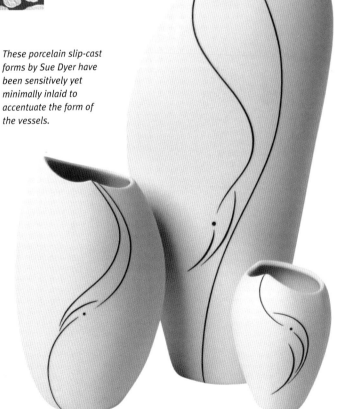

SEE ALSO:

Making models,
130–131

MOULD MAKING

Plaster moulds are very useful if you want to be able to reproduce a shape exactly that cannot easily be made by hand building or throwing. Don't be daunted by the prospect of mixing plaster – if you weigh and measure your ingredients properly and follow some simple steps there is very little that can go wrong.

Fail-safe plaster recipe

You will need

Tools and equipment:
• Bucket or large bowl
• Measuring jug
• Scoop
• Weighing scales
• Newspaper

Plaster : water ratio =
675 g (1 1/2 lb)
plaster : 575 ml
(1 pint) water

This will give a strong enough mix for most pottery uses. For a harder mix, increase the plaster by 0.1 kg (1/4 lb). This is more suitable for multipart moulds that will be used repeatedly.

1 Measure the required amount of water into a bowl, then weigh out the relevant quantity of plaster. Carefully sprinkle all the plaster into the water until it breaks the surface. Gently shake the container until all the plaster seeps down into the water.

• Always add the plaster to water – never the other way around.
• When mixing plaster it is essential that you have enough to cover the model for your mould completely, otherwise you will get visible lines in the mould that will show up later in clay, especially if you are slip casting.
• It is better to overestimate an amount of plaster than have too little – if you don't want to be wasteful simply make a few sprig models to use up any surplus. Alternatively, use the excess to make a texture bat (see page 130).
• Plaster is contaminating – never allow plaster bits to get into your clay because it will cause damage to your pots in firing. Try to keep a separate area in your workshop for plaster work and be meticulous when cleaning up after making moulds.

• When you are mixing plaster, scoop the bubbles off the surface and into a prelined container. This will make disposal of the excess much easier. Keep the container handy to dispose of any mixture left over that you cannot use after making your mould.
• Never pour excess plaster down the sink – it will set and block the pipes! Clean excess plaster from your hands with newspaper before washing them to avoid blockages.
• Use newspaper to clean out the plaster bucket immediately after use.
• Wear rubber or latex gloves to mix plaster if your skin is sensitive.
• Wear a facemask when mixing plaster if you are concerned about inhaling dust.

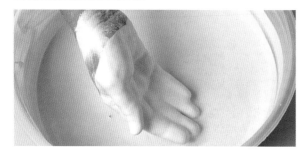

2 Stir the mixture gently with your hand to remove any lumps – every so often wiggle your hand at the bottom of the mixture to release trapped air bubbles. Scoop off the bubbles that collect at the top of the mixture. The mixture is ready when it no longer runs off your fingers and is obviously thickening. This can happen relatively quickly, or it may take several minutes.

239

How to contain the plaster

A cottle is a retaining wall that is built up around a model to contain the plaster. The shape of the model it surrounds dictates the material the cottle is made from.

Linoleum

Linoleum is a cheap and flexible cottle material that can easily be cut to size, is reusable and does not require soaping.

Soft clay

Soft clay is generally used for small moulding walls – sprig moulds, knobs, handles and so on – and does not require soaping.

Wooden boards

These boards were salvaged from a set of drawers and are plastic coated, so do not need soaping. Melamine boards are good for the same reason, but if you cannot find anything similar use marine ply, which is relatively resistant to water. For ease of release, soap marine ply before use. Most pottery suppliers have adjustable wooden frames for mould making but it is not worth buying one unless you intend to make a lot of moulds!

Plaster bats

Plaster bats can be made in the same way as texture bats, but without the texture, and are easily cut to the required size. They will need soaping before use to avoid sticking to the freshly poured plaster.

Sizing up

"Sizing up" is the term used to describe the preparation of absorbent surfaces with soap size prior to plaster casting. Here is the method for sizing a plaster model. (Wooden surfaces should be sized in the same way, but do not need to be soaked first.)

1 Soak the model for about 15 minutes in clean water to saturate the plaster.

2 Using a soft bristle brush, soap over the surface of the model.

3 Wipe away all traces of soap that remain with a dampened natural sponge.

4 Repeat the process three more times, then buff up the surface with a dry, clean soft brush to remove all traces of soap.

TRY IT

240 **Materials for securing cottles**

- **Clothes pegs:** Useful for holding lino cottles together before securing them with string.
- **String:** Varying lengths of strong string, preferably nylon with a knot at one end and a loop at the other for easy tying.
- **Masking or gaffer tape:** Can be used instead of string.
- **Soft clay:** For sealing seams on the outside of cottles to prevent plaster escaping.
- **Wooden wedges:** Help to keep string taut when using wooden boards as a cottle.

FIX IT

241 **Can't separate your plaster from the mould?**

Any absorbent surface must be sealed with soap "size" prior to casting in plaster – otherwise they will never be separated. The size forms a skin or barrier between the surfaces and is vitally important for success. You'll need the following materials:
- **Mould maker's size or soft soap:** Available from your pottery supplier, it usually comes in a solidified or thick form and needs diluting with an equal amount of boiling water.
- **Soft bristle brushes:** For applying soap size and buffing up.
- **Natural sponges:** Use them dampened to remove excess soap.

SEE ALSO:
Mould making,
128–129

Making models

Models for casting in plaster can be made from a variety of materials – including plaster itself – but also clay, modelling clay, wood, Perspex or Styrofoam. The choice of material depends on the type of finish you require. For instance, sharp angles are best achieved using wood, Perspex or plaster. Softer angled forms would be better made from clay or modelling clay.

The method for making a texture bat

1 Build a low wall around the texture you have chosen – in this case, vinyl wallpaper, but see opposite for more ideas. Use strips of wooden batten that have been cut so that they locate over one another to form a frame.

If you use battens, they should be no less than 1.2 cm (1/2 in) thick.

2 The amount of plaster you need will depend on the size of your frame. Mix more than you think you will need and prepare another model just in case you have too much.

Pour the plaster into the frame until it just breaks over the top edges.

3 When all the plaster is in the frame, "shiver" your hand over the surface to release any remaining air bubbles. Tapping the board up and down gently will have the same effect. (This procedure applies when making any mould.)

4 With the ends sitting firmly on the wooden frame draw a metal ruler across the surface of the bat to remove any excess plaster and ensure the bat is flat.

5 When the plaster has set remove the frame carefully, then remove sharp edges on the underside of the bat with a fine blade. Keep the edges on the textured side sharp and crisp. Put the bat in a warm place to dry out – preferably elevated so that air can move around it freely. Supported on props on top of the kiln is a good place.

Making a texture bat

The easiest way to introduce yourself to plaster work is by making simple texture bats that can be cut and reconstructed to make moulds. This technique will enable you to get the practice required for mixing plaster correctly, while also learning the procedures for making moulds successfully.

243

Texture suggestions

Vinyl wallpaper
Vinyl wallpaper is available in a wide range of patterns and is often reusable – ask for samples from a DIY store rather than buying whole rolls; you will be surprised how long they last. Tape a piece of blown vinyl wallpaper securely to a non-absorbent board.

Stamps
You can make your own textured slabs using stamps. These stamps are a mixture of found objects and handmade wooden, clay and plaster blocks. Try old earrings, buttons, beads or shells. Almost anything will make a mark in clay.

Texture rollers
Look out for these decorative plaster rollers used in interior decoration; they make great textures and you can make large slabs really quickly. Alternately, make your own texture rollers from old rolling pins (see page 26).

Organic materials
Try rolling leaves or flowers into clay. Choose samples with interesting shapes and outlines, and good veining on the undersides to make distinct impressions. Also try seed heads, bark, or seaweed – all work well. Remove the leaves carefully with a pin before casting in plaster.

Lace
Lace makes a good alternative to wallpaper, but make sure it is stretched taut before taping it down to keep it from rippling when the plaster is poured over it. Alternately, roll lace into a slab of clay – when it is removed, it leaves a pattern in the clay that can then be cast in plaster.

244

Putting the bats together for casting

1 When your bats have dried out, measure and cut them into narrower blocks for a four-sided vessel. They can be equally sized for a square, or two sides may be narrower for a rectangular vessel, but all should be the same height. You will need a saw to cut the plaster.

2 Stand the plaster sections together on a plain plaster base to form a four-sided vessel with the texture on the inside. They should stand easily without falling apart if you have neatened the edges properly.

3 Wrap some string around the mould several times and tie it firmly, then push a wedge of wood between the string and plaster on each side to keep the string taut.

4 Seal all joined edges on the outside of the mould with coils of very soft clay. It may help to dip the coils in water before applying them. Your mould is now ready for slip casting. Once you have mastered the technique of constructing simple shapes, try making

some with more than four sides – or vessels with angled walls instead of straight ones. It will require a bit more planning to cut the angles correctly, but with some experimentation you will find you can make many different forms.

245

How to make a symmetrical press mould

1 Draw an accurate outline shape to your required dimensions on a sheet of stiff card. The sides must be equilateral for the shape to work when it is made in clay. Cut the shape out carefully. (See the Decorative wares directory on pages 148–153 for outline ideas.)

2 Draw and cut out a top and bottom section as shown, to the depth you would like your pot to be.

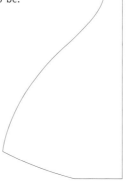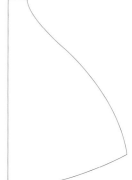

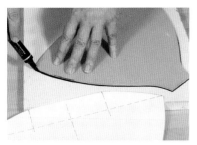

3 Transfer the design to a non-absorbent board by drawing around the outline with a marker pen.

4 Fill in the outline shape with soft clay. Smoothing it over as you build up the level will help you to define the shape. The form should rise gently from the sides to the middle. When the outline shape has been completely filled in, smooth off the clay along the bottom edge so that it is vertical and there are no undercuts.

5 Position the base section of card against this edge and, holding it in place with one hand, carefully scrape away the excess clay from the body of the model using a kidney, to define the shape at the lower edge.

6 Repeat the procedure for the top end of the model using the smaller cutout section of card to define the shape as for the base. Finish the model by working over the surface with a metal kidney to perfect the shape, then a rubber kidney to smooth it. The model is now ready for cottling up and casting in plaster.

246

Making turned clay models

You can make clay models in a number of ways, but one of the quickest methods is to turn one from a centred lump of clay on a wheel. This method is especially suitable for making one-piece press-mould bowl forms, where the shape needs to be perfectly round. See the Decorative wares directory on pages 146–151 for ideas.

Casting hump moulds

Use your press moulds as models from which to make hump moulds.

1 Soap-size your press mould (see page 129), then gently fill the mould with plaster.

2 When the plaster has set but not dried, score grooves into the surface with a sharp tool.

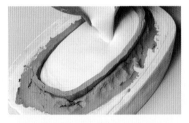

3 Build a clay wall about 5 cm (2 in) deep around the scored central section of plaster, and secure it in place with very soft clay. Fill the enclosed area with more plaster.

4 Remove the clay wall when the plaster has set, scrape the bottom of the riser, and soften the plaster edges with a thin blade. Separate the moulds carefully then use the blade on the edge of the mould as before.

Removing models from moulds

Do:
• Ease the model gently out of the mould to avoid breaking delicate edges. This applies to any type of model.
• Wipe away all traces of clay from the mould with a damp sponge after removing a clay model. This is not necessary for all moulds.

Don't:
• Use sharp tools to dig clay models out of moulds; they can easily damage the surface of the mould.

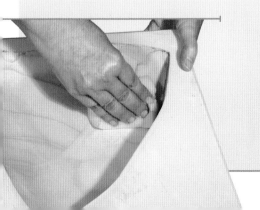

Model-making tips

• If you centre and trim your model on a wooden bat, then it can remain in place to cast in plaster. However, remember that you will need to soap the board up before casting.
• The most important consideration when turning models is that there should be no undercuts – this would make it impossible to remove the plaster mould.
• Allow at least 2.5 cm (1 in) around a model when building a cottle to contain plaster. The walls of the cottle should be sealed to the bat with a coil of soft clay so that no plaster can run out.

FIX IT

248 **Underestimated the amount of plaster you need?**

When you are making a mould it is essential that the model is covered with plaster in one go – providing you have mixed enough to achieve this much, all is not lost. Simply follow these steps to rectify the problem:

After pouring the first batch of plaster, wait for it to set. Score the surface with a sharp tool. Be very careful if the first covering is very thin that you do not score through to the model beneath. Mix a second batch of plaster and pour it over the first. The scored lines will "key" the two mixes together.

249
Using found objects as models

You can use almost anything as a model to cast in plaster, but when you are starting to make moulds it is easier to look for simple shapes that you would like to reproduce in clay – the kitchen is a good place to start. The most important consideration when choosing a model to make a mould from is that it has no undercuts.

Found object tips

• Look in charity shops and boot sales for unusual items to use as models.
• Also look for old lace and unusual textured fabrics for rolling into clay – you will be amazed what you can find for very little money!

Fixing holes

If you find holes in the mould caused by bubbles in the plaster, fill them in by first spraying them with water then carefully sprinkling plaster into them until they are full. When the plaster begins to set, scrape over the area with a kidney or modelling tool to smooth the surface back to the same level as the rest of the mould.

Undercuts would make this model impossible to release from the mould. To solve the problem, the model should be embedded in clay up to the dotted line. The upper section can then be added on at the making stage using another method like coiling.

250
Successful press and hump moulds

Press moulds

If you are making a press mould from a bowl you will need to seal the bowl onto a board before casting to prevent plaster getting underneath. You can do this with a flattened coil of soft clay. Level the clay carefully before cottling up because this will form the rim of the mould. Soap-size the model if you are concerned about it releasing after casting.

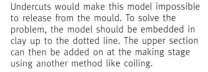

Hump moulds

Choose shallow vessels to make hump moulds from and follow the same procedure as shown for making plaster models on page 133.

251
How to add your own drawn designs

You can draw designs into plaster moulds that will stand out in relief in clay. This technique is most suitable for hump molds where the design will be seen on the inside of the form. Score the design while the plaster is still soft enough using a pointed modeling tool, and remove the plaster bits with a soft brush as you work.

252
Making irregular forms and undercuts

A two-part mould (see opposite) allows you to produce an irregularly shaped form that may have simple undercuts because joints in the mould allow the two parts to be removed in different directions. If you are pressing the form, the two halves must be pressed individually then joined together by scoring and slipping. You can make slip-cast forms in one go by making a pouring hole in the mould for the slip.

253

Making a two-part mould for pressing from a found object

A pear is used to make a two-part mould in this example. However, the making technique is the same for any object, providing the shape is not so irregular that there are too many undercuts.

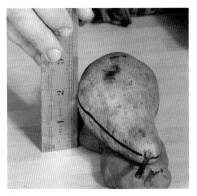

1 Draw a line around the model with a marker pen to mark the halfway position. Use a triangle to do this if it helps.

2 Use soft clay to fill in any areas that would create obvious problems of undercuts. Here the bottom is too indented, so it is levelled off with the clay.

3 Balance the model on a pad of soft clay; then, using a ruler to measure the height to the marker line, make adjustments until it is the same height and level all the way around.

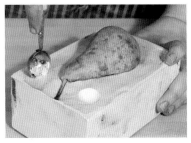

4 Embed the lower half of the model in clay up to the marker line. Ideally there should be 2.5–3.2 cm (1–1 1/2 in) of clay surrounding it. Level and smooth the clay bed, taking great care around the model itself. Build a cottle around the embedded model, then cast in plaster.

5 When the plaster has set, remove the cottle and the clay from around the model but leave the model itself in place in the plaster.

6 Clean the surface around the object with a damp sponge to remove any traces of clay, then cut a "natch" into each corner, using either a melon scoop or a penny. To make a natch with a penny, simply hold it between your finger and thumb, then rotate the edge into the plaster. It will make a perfect little hole.

7 Size up the surface of the plaster with the model still in place (see page 133), making sure to include the natch holes, then cottle up the sides again and cast the second half.

8 When the mould has been separated remove the model and tidy the outer edges with a thin blade, taking care not to alter the shape.

Making a two-part mould for slip casting

The only difference between this type of mould and the last one is that it needs a pouring hole for the slip. The position of the hole is dictated by the use of the form you are making. See Making spares on page 137 for more details.

254 More model ideas

You can use a variety of other materials as models for one- or two-part moulds.
• **Plastic drainpipe:** This is great for making two-part cylindrical forms. It is available in several widths and can easily be cut to sizes of your choice. It does not need sizing up.
• **Old rolling pins:** The types with removable handles are the best, again for cylindrical forms.

• **Timber blocks:** These are good for making moulds for slip casting. The wood should be smooth and unmarked.
• **Wood or MDF board:** Look for offcuts of thick board at the DIY store and mitre the edges if you have access to the correct machinery. These make great moulds for shallow dishes.

TRY IT

255 Moulds from materials other than plaster

Try some of these simple alternatives to plaster moulds:
• Ridge tiles for roofs make great hump moulds for dishes, or can be used for moulding slabs to construct pots. They are available in a number of different shapes.
• Make a sling mould from an upturned chair by tying a square of fabric to the four legs. When a slab of clay is placed in the centre, the shape will drape according to how taut the fabric is. Leave the clay in place until it has stiffened enough to handle.
• Use inflated balloons as hump moulds; just make sure the balloon is securely fixed down before draping your slabs over it. Sitting the balloon in a bowl works well and draping a piece of cloth over the surface before draping the clay will prevent sticking.

256 Unsticking moulds

If your mould will not come apart easily after you have cast the second half, place a soft cloth over the surface of the mould then place a weight or heavy object on top. Now give the weight a few taps with another weight and the mould should easily pop apart – if not, try again in another position.

For moulds that are really stuck: allow the mould to dry out somewhat, then stand it in the sink with the join side uppermost, and pour boiling water over it. As the plaster contracts, the mould should spring apart. Remove the model then dry the mould with the sections together.

257

Making spares

The "spare" is usually an extension of clay or plaster which forms the opening of the mould through which the slip is poured. If there were no spare, the rim of the cast would be very uneven.

Once the spare has been fitted in place, the model is prepared for casting in the same way as for the two-part mould for pressing – except that one cottle wall must butt directly up to the spare end of the model so that when cast, it will remain open.

Other things you can utilize to make spares:

- Bottle corks
- Modelling clay
- Styrofoam

The spare

Preparing the model for casting

258

Moulding fine details

"Sprig moulds" are really a form of decoration because they are applied to the surface of a form to provide low-relief detail. They are made in exactly the same way as other types of mould but on a much smaller scale.

If you find it too difficult to model fine detail into a small sprig, scale the sprig up to a manageable size then dry and fire it – either to biscuit or the clay's top temperature depending on the reduction in size required. You can then cast the sprig in plaster with all the detail in place.

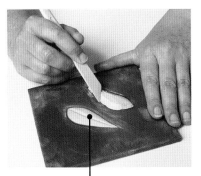

Clay models for sprigs must be carefully modelled to avoid undercuts.

Natural forms will need to be embedded in clay before casting, to avoid undercuts.

259

Making a mould from a wooden block

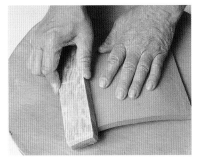

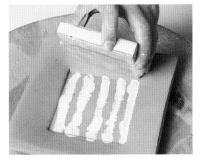

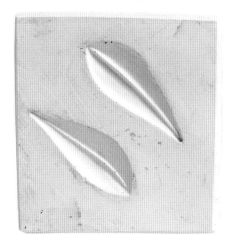

1 Use a straight-sided wooden block as a mould. Simply drape a slab of clay over the block, then press the sides down to touch the baseboard.

2 Allow the clay to stiffen before inverting the dish to reveal a crisp square outline in the centre. Try wooden blocks with more than four sides for interestingly shaped dishes.

SEE ALSO:

Slabbing,
40–41
Coiling,
72–73

Getting more from moulds

Moulds give you great versatility for personal expression
in clay because they can be used in so many possible ways.
Try the ideas on the following pages to get you started.

260

Start with a simple slab

1 A simple slab is the simplest way
of using a mould. Press the slab
carefully into one half of the mould
using a damp sponge to ease it into
place. Repeat with another slab to fill
the second half of the mould.

2 Remove excess clay from the rim
with one of your roller guides held
flat against the surface. You could
use a ruler, or any other flat tool, but
don't use a knife; it will cut into the
plaster and contaminate the clay.

Never try to press a whole slab of
clay into a deep mould – it will buckle
and tear. Instead, cut the slab into
manageable sections and position them
so that they overlay one another in the
mould. You can then blend the surfaces
together with a thumb or finger before
smoothing over with a kidney.

3 When you have turned your vessel
out of the mould, reinforce the joins
on the outside with a coil of soft
clay, then smooth over with a kidney.

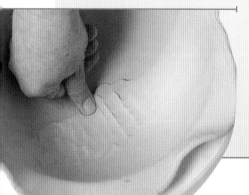

261

Adding to moulded forms

Basic moulded forms can be
added to in several ways – try
the following:

Flattened coils

Follow the method for making
flattened coils on page 72. Score
and slip the rim of the bowl before
joining on the coil. Reinforce the
joins with soft clay. Scrape away
the excess with a kidney.

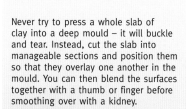

Rounded coils

Use small rounded coils to extend
the height or shape of a moulded
base in a decorative way. Build up a
design by bending and twisting coils
into different shapes and patterns.
Use small balls of clay to fill in
spaces. Blend all the coils together
thoroughly on the inside of the pot
before scraping the surface smooth
with a kidney. You could use little
stamps to add extra decorative detail
to coils added onto moulded bases.

Moulding textured slabs

You can use textured slabs in moulds if you are careful, but choose moulds that are not too deep because you cannot blend sections in the mould for this technique. Otherwise, make a form where only half a section of clay is required, as in this walled vessel.

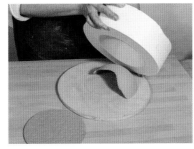

1 Press the slab very gently into the mould, texture side down. Use a damp sponge to ease it into place, but do not press too hard otherwise the texture will be squashed. Finish the mould as you would for the plain slab version.

2 Moulded sections like these can be joined onto flat slabs that have been textured in the same way. The flat slab can be any shape, but here it has been cut to the same size as the moulded section.

Texture tip

When using textured slabs in this way try using the natural edge of the slab as it has been rolled to form the opening of the moulded part of the vessel, rather than a cut edge. It gives the form a more organic look.

The finished form

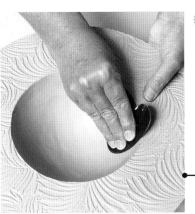

Extending the basic form

• If the rim is wide compared to the moulded section of your form, dry and biscuit-fire it upside down to keep it flat. Make sure the two sections are fixed together well and reinforced on the underside with coils of soft clay.

• Foot rings and handles can be made and added using any of the making techniques, including thrown sections. The key factor to remember is that the clay section to be added on should be the same thickness as the moulded section, no matter what technique you use to make it.

Try using textured slabs to make extended rims on moulded forms.

Coiling inside moulds

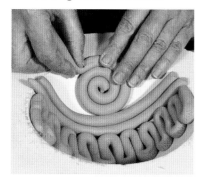 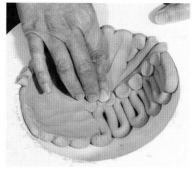

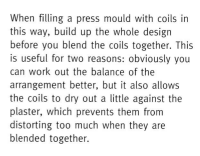

When filling a press mould with coils in this way, build up the whole design before you blend the coils together. This is useful for two reasons: obviously you can work out the balance of the arrangement better, but it also allows the coils to dry out a little against the plaster, which prevents them from distorting too much when they are blended together.

Coils can be used in a number of ways to great decorative effect in both hump and press moulds.

You may find it easier to build up the pattern of coils on the work surface before placing them in the mould. Work on a non-absorbent surface to avoid the coils drying out too much.

Once you are happy with the arrangement of coils, blend them together very thoroughly without squashing the clay too much then carefully scrape the surface back to smooth with a kidney.

Coiling over moulds

The same rules for construction apply when applying coils over hump moulds. Add flattened coils to form the rims and frame the design and a few stamp marks to finish off.

The three designs shown here show the potential for creating endless varieties of patterns using coils in this way. You could finish off the dish by making simple coiled feet for the underside to give the form some lift.

266

Weaving coils in a mould

Clay coils for weaving should be quite soft, and should contain a medium-sized grog for strength. Prepare all the coils in advance – you will have to work quickly, as the plaster will draw water from the coils. Keep your coils under plastic until you use them. Work from the centre out, squarely. Lay the first coil over the centre of the mould, with the second over the top to form a cross. Place the third coil next to the first and over the second. Fit the fourth coil over the third and under the first. The fifth coil goes under the fourth and over the second, and so on until the surface is covered. Attach a final flattened coil to frame the form and hold it all together.

Woven forms are more easily worked over simple hump moulds but can be made in press moulds with practice. This type of form can be quite vulnerable to handle after making so take care and support the form as it dries to keep the shape.

267

Press moulding in two parts

The same rules apply for pressing clay in moulds with two parts as for one-piece moulds, but with a few additional considerations.

1 Ease the clay into the mould gently using a damp sponge rather than your fingers. If you feel the clay has stretched and may be a little thin in places, reinforce it with some soft clay, blended in well to even out the thickness.

2 When both halves of the mould have been pressed, score and slip the edges to be joined with water and a toothbrush.

3 Close the two halves of the mould tightly together and leave for a minute or two for the joins to seal.

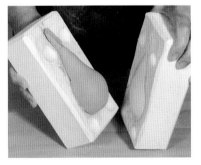

4 When you open the mould again, the form will remain in one half – ease it out carefully.

5 Smooth over the join with a kidney to make sure it is thoroughly sealed, then neaten up any little details that require it.

FIX IT

268 **How do I stop hollow forms exploding?**

When making hollow forms that are completely sealed, you must pierce a hole somewhere inconspicuous before firing to allow the escape of air – otherwise the form could explode as the air heats and expands inside.

269

Adapting basic forms

Decorative forms can easily be made into functional items by altering and adding a few small details.

Sugar or jam pot

Cut the form into two to make a lidded pot. You can make a locating ring just inside the lid from a thin strip of slabbed clay or a coil. Cut a hole large enough for a spoon that bisects the lid and bottom section. You can even model a spoon to fit the pot if you want to!

Oil bottle

Cut only a very small lid for this form, and add a longish plug of clay to the inside of the lid to act as a locater and also to prevent the lid falling off when the oil is poured. Make a hole in the side of the form for the spout to fit over, then make a spout from a thin slab of clay wrapped around a paintbrush or similar tool. Reinforce the join around the spout and blend in well. Add a little coil handle to finish.

270

Slip casting

Slip casting is the technique of pouring liquid slip into a mould to make a form in one piece. Casting slips are available ready to use from your pottery supplier and these are the best option by far if you are just beginning.

Slip type	Casting time	Firing temperature
White earthenware	*20–30 minutes*	*1000–1150°C (1832–2102°F)*
Red earthenware	*20–30 minutes*	*1000–1150°C (1832–2102°F)*
Stoneware	*45 minutes–1 hour*	*1160–1290°C (2120–2354°F)*
Semi-porcelain/ high-firing white earthenware	*20–30 minutes*	*1100–1260°C (2012–2300°F)*
Porcelain	*5–10 minutes*	*1260–1280°C (2300–2336°F)*
Bone china*	*2–7 minutes*	*1220–1260°C (2228–2300°F)*

* Bone china is not a slip to choose when starting out because it requires special firing treatments and is notoriously difficult to handle! If you have no experience with slip *casting, start with white earthenware because it is easy to cast and fire and is the cheapest option for experimentation.*

Slip casting in different moulds

The process for slip casting into any mould is basically the same as for casting in the texture mould (see opposite), although you will need to take care when casting shallow open forms because they can more easily drop out as the slip dries. This is why moulds are made with spares; the spare acts as a point to cast to and prevents the form from dropping out when it is inverted to drain.

271

Slip casting into a texture mould

1 Stir your casting slip thoroughly until it is a good pouring consistency, then fill your mould as full as possible. Leave the slip in the mould for the recommended time. You will notice the level of the slip dropping as the water is sucked into the plaster, so top it up occasionally to keep it full.

2 Pour the slip out of the mould carefully. Rotating the mould as you pour will help to keep the thickness of the walls even, but only do this if you can manage it easily.

3 Support the mould upside down on two wooden battens so the remainder of the slip can drip out. Leave the mould like this until it has stopped dripping, then turn it back over and leave it until the clay is firm enough to hold its shape.

5 A form like this needs only the minimal amount of fettling (see page 144) to avoid spoiling the neat edges. Simply break off any unsightly bits from the seams – don't wipe with a damp sponge! Any sharp areas can be lightly sanded after biscuit firing and before glazing.

4 Remove the plaster bat walls carefully but leave the form on the base bat until it is completely dry.

TRY IT

272 **Casting a two-part mould with a spare**

This mould has been cast and processed in exactly the same way as the texture mould, but here you can see that before the mould is opened the spare is cut away with a knife to leave a neat rim on the form.

SEE ALSO:

Getting more
from moulds,
138–143

Fettling

"Fettling" is the term used to describe the process of neatening and finishing off the outside of a slip-cast form. This process is best done when the form is completely dry and only applies to slip-cast forms.

---

273 | **Neatening seams**

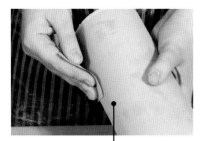

Use wet and dry paper to remove the seam lines on your forms, or...

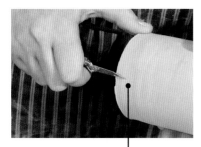

... scrape the surface gently with a knife or kidney to remove irregularities.

274 | **Making levelling easy**

1 Make a great but simple tool for levelling the bottoms of slip-cast forms by stretching and stapling a sheet of chamois leather over a board.

2 To use the board, simply pour some water over the chamois then move the pot over the surface in a circular action until the base feels flat. You can do the same for rims but these are much more vulnerable, so take care.

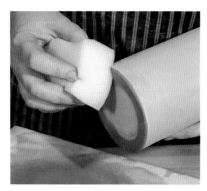

3 Remove any slurry that has accumulated around the rim with a damp sponge.

TRY IT

Sponge on a stick

Use a sponge on a stick to neaten rims or other areas that are difficult to reach.

Shellac resist

Shellac flakes are available from furniture makers and suppliers. Make the mixture by putting the flakes in a screwtop container, then covering with enough methylated spirits to form a slightly thickened liquid. It may take a little while for the flakes to dissolve – and a little goes a long way – so only make small amounts at a time.

1 Slip cast some plain tiles to practise on and allow them to dry out completely. Draw your design onto the tile then carefully paint the shellac inside the shapes. Keep the design simple to begin with.

2 Allow the shellac to dry completely, then wash away the clay around the painted areas with a dampened sponge. If the clay appears to be getting too saturated allow it to dry completely, then repeat the process again until you are happy with the result.

3 The shellac burns away when the tile is fired, leaving the design standing out in relief on the surface. You can leave this surface unglazed and fire the tile up to its top temperature, or glaze as you would any other surface. This not an easy technique for the beginner to master, but it creates such lovely surfaces on fine clays that it is worth persevering, if only to create a design on a small area of your form.

Monoprinting from plaster

1 Paint a design with coloured slips directly onto the plaster inside both halves of a two-part mould, before slip casting in the usual way.

Porcelain casting slips are available in several different colours, so try:

• Dribbling a few different colours into the mould before casting the form up as usual – this gives a more abstract finish.
• Slip-trailing a design into the mould for a more precise pattern.
• Casting successive thin layers of different coloured slips into a mould then, when it is completely dry, wipe through the layers with a damp sponge until all the colours have been revealed. You can do this randomly or in an ordered way to form a pattern. Take care not to wipe away too much, and if the clay appears to be getting saturated allow it to dry again before continuing.

2 When the form comes out of the mould, the design will be inlaid into the body. Allow it to dry before fettling.

Slip-cast decoration

Slip-cast forms are suitable for glazing in the same way that any other clay form would be, but not all decorative techniques are appropriate for this type of ware.

Multiple layers of coloured-bone china casting slip were thinly poured into plaster moulds to make these bowls (left) by Sasha Wardell. After allowing to dry to leather-hard, small slices were cut from the walls to reveal the colours beneath.

Chapter 4

Useful information

On the pages that follow you can find a collection of ideas for profiles for bowls, vases, hollow wares, spouts and lips, and even animal shapes. The profiles are all keyed in to the most suitable making methods. Use the profile ideas as they are or adapt them to your own designs. There is also a glossary of all the technical terms used in the book.

Decorative wares directory

These diagrams showing different decorative forms can be used in several ways: as a source of inspiration when you are lost for something to make, to create formers or guides for coil building or as a basis for templates for soft slabbed forms.

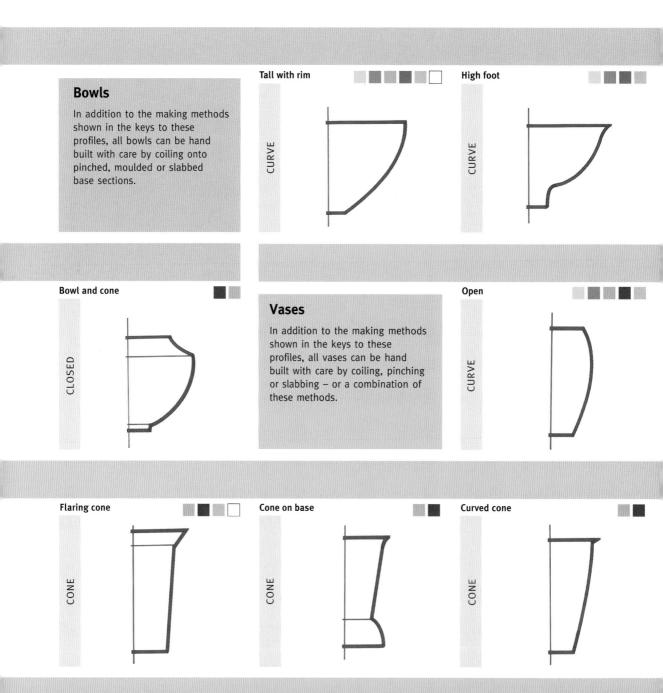

Bowls

In addition to the making methods shown in the keys to these profiles, all bowls can be hand built with care by coiling onto pinched, moulded or slabbed base sections.

Tall with rim

CURVE

High foot

CURVE

Bowl and cone

CLOSED

Vases

In addition to the making methods shown in the keys to these profiles, all vases can be hand built with care by coiling, pinching or slabbing – or a combination of these methods.

Open

CURVE

Flaring cone

CONE

Cone on base

CONE

Curved cone

CONE

HOW TO USE THE DIRECTORY

To make outline formers: photocopy and enlarge the diagrams to the size you require, then transfer the image to hardboard or thin MDF (medium-desity fibreboard). To make templates for slabbed forms, simply draw the shape as a mirror copy to form a complete outline.

The examples over the next few pages offer guidance for suitable making methods and clays to use but these are by no means definitive – use them experimentally to stretch your creativity.

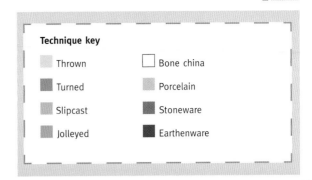

Technique key

- Thrown
- Turned
- Slipcast
- Jolleyed
- Bone china
- Porcelain
- Stoneware
- Earthenware

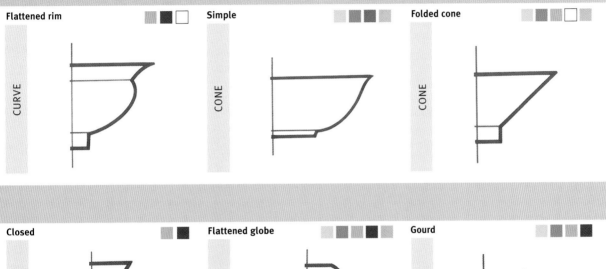

Flattened rim — CURVE

Simple — CONE

Folded cone — CONE

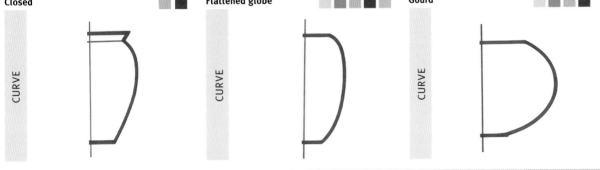

Closed — CURVE

Flattened globe — CURVE

Gourd — CURVE

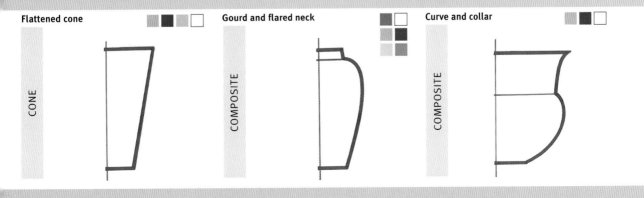

Flattened cone — CONE

Gourd and flared neck — COMPOSITE

Curve and collar — COMPOSITE

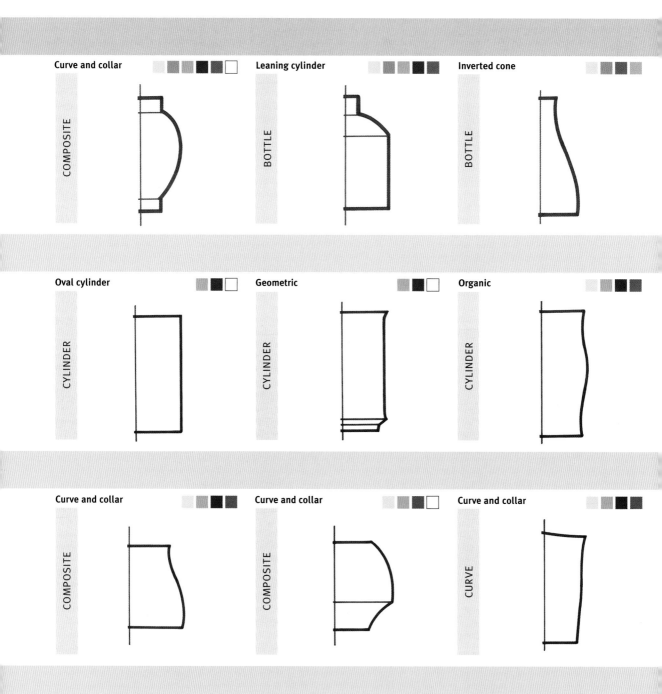

Curve and collar

COMPOSITE

Leaning cylinder

BOTTLE

Inverted cone

BOTTLE

Oval cylinder

CYLINDER

Geometric

CYLINDER

Organic

CYLINDER

Curve and collar

COMPOSITE

Curve and collar

COMPOSITE

Curve and collar

CURVE

Hollow wares

Jugs – both large and small – can be made using hand building techniques with care. The keys suggest the simplest methods of making, but the choice is always a matter of personal preference. These outlines would also make suitable shapes for vases.

Pear shape

CURVE

Simple curve

CURVE

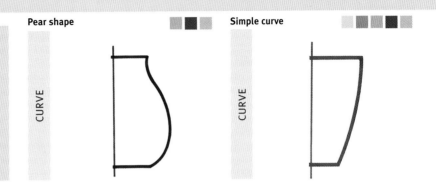

Organic

CYLINDER

Tall baluster

COMPOSITE

Gourd and collar

COMPOSITE

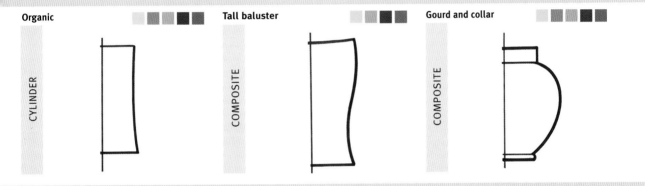

Globe and collar

CURVE

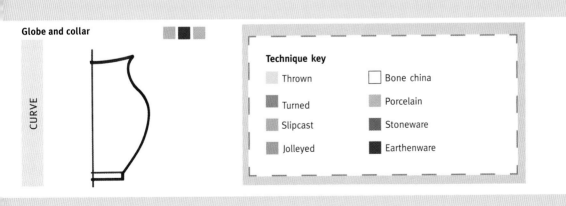

Technique key

Thrown	Bone china
Turned	Porcelain
Slipcast	Stoneware
Jolleyed	Earthenware

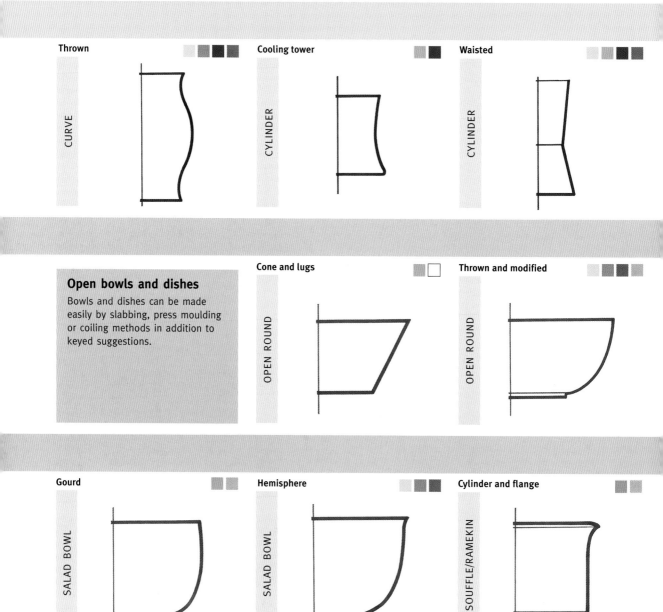

Thrown

CURVE

Cooling tower

CYLINDER

Waisted

CYLINDER

Open bowls and dishes

Bowls and dishes can be made easily by slabbing, press moulding or coiling methods in addition to keyed suggestions.

Cone and lugs

OPEN ROUND

Thrown and modified

OPEN ROUND

Gourd

SALAD BOWL

Hemisphere

SALAD BOWL

Cylinder and flange

SOUFFLE/RAMEKIN

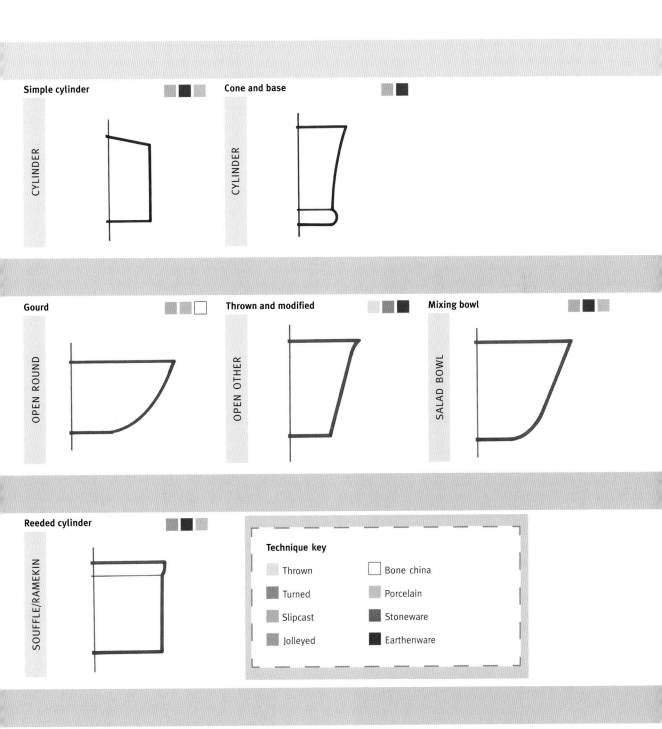

Simple cylinder

CYLINDER

Cone and base

CYLINDER

Gourd

OPEN ROUND

Thrown and modified

OPEN OTHER

Mixing bowl

SALAD BOWL

Reeded cylinder

SOUFFLE/RAMEKIN

Technique key

Thrown

Turned

Slipcast

Jolleyed

Bone china

Porcelain

Stoneware

Earthenware

Glossary

Altering
Pots thrown on the wheel are round and symmetrical, but can be altered by exerting gentle pressure with the palms to create oval shapes. The rims of bottles and even bowls can be altered in this way.

Ash
Useful ingredient as the fluxing agent of a glaze. Wood ash is usual, but coal ash, and any plant ash, is also usable. Ash also may have a high silica content, and combined with clay it will form a simple stoneware glaze.

Ball clay
Clay of high plasticity, high firing and pale in colour. An ingredient of throwing clay and other bodies as well as glazes.

Banding wheel
A turntable operated by hand, used for decorating purposes.

Bat
A plaster or wooden disc for throwing pots on, moving pots without handling or for the drying of clay.

Biscuit/bisque
First low-temperature firing to which a pot is subjected. Moisture within the clay is driven off slowly in the form of steam, along with other organic compounds – clay becomes converted to "pot", a chemical change that is irreversible. Biscuit firing is usually between 850°–1000°C (1562°F and 1832°F) but can be higher if less porosity is required. Work is often biscuit fired before being decorated in various ways.

Body
The term used to describe a particular mixture of clay such as stoneware body and porcelain body.

Bone china
A clay body with a quantity of bone ash in the recipe.

Carborundum stone
A hard, dense stone used for grinding away rough patches on fired ceramic. Carborundum paper is used in the same way.

Casting
Making pots by pouring slip into a porous mould to build up a layer of clay.

Casting slip
A liquid clay used in the process of forming objects with moulds. Also referred to simply as slip.

Chuck
A hollow form made in clay or plaster that holds a pot securely during turning.

Cobalt oxide/carbonate (CoO and CoCO3)
Powerful blue colourants. Used widely in ancient China, cobalt is said to have been first found in Persia. Blue and white decoration is one of the strongest traditions in ceramics.

Coiling
Making pots using coils or ropes of clay.

Collaring
The action of squeezing around a pot in order to draw the shape inwards.

Cones/pyrometric cones
Compressed glaze material formulated to bend at designated temperatures. The structures are placed in the kiln where they can be seen through the spyhole. They provide an accurate indicator of the "heat-work" of the firing i.e. the real effectiveness of temperature and time on the clay and glazes.

Copper oxide/carbonate (CuCO3)
Strong colourant in ceramics giving green to black and brown. Under certain reduction conditions it can also give a blood red.

Decals
Pictures or text printed onto special transfer paper; used to decorate pottery.

Deflocculant
An alkaline substance, commonly sodium silicate or soda ash, which is added to a slip to make the mixture more fluid without the addition of water. The clay particles remain dispersed and in suspension, an essential quality required for casting. Also see Flocculant.

Earthenware
Pottery fired to a relatively low temperature. The body remains porous and usually requires a glaze if it is to be used for containing water or food.

Elements
The metal heating coils in an electric kiln.

Enamels
Low-temperature colours containing fluxes, usually applied on top of a fired glaze. Enamels require a further firing to render them permanent. Also known as on-glaze colours or china paints.

Engobe
Prepared slip that contains some fluxing ingredient. It lies halfway between a clay slip and a glaze.

Fettling
Term used when cast ware is trimmed and sponged to remove excess clay and seams. Fettling is done at the leather-hard or dry stage.

Firing
The process by which ceramic ware is heated in a kiln to bring glaze or clay to maturity.

Flocculant
An acid or salt which when added to slip has a thickening effect and aids suspension, delaying settlement. Calcium chloride and vinegar are commonly used as flocculants.

Flux
An essential glaze ingredient that lowers the melting point of silica, the glass-making ingredient. A number of oxides serve as fluxes, each having its own characteristic.

Foot
The base of a piece of pottery on which it rests.

Foot ring
The circle of clay at the base of a pot that raises the form from the surface it is standing on.

Frit
Material used in low temperature glazes. Frits are made by heating and fusing certain materials together, after which they are finely ground to a powder. In this way, soluble or toxic substances can be stabilized and made safe to use.

Fused
Melted together, but not necessarily vitrified.

Glaze
Super-cooled liquid of glass-like nature that is fused to the surface of the pot.

Grog
A ceramic material, usually clay, that has been heated to a high temperature before use. Usually added to clay to lessen warping and increase its resistance to thermal shock.

Iron oxide
The most common and versatile colouring oxide, used in many slips and glazes and often present in clays, too. Red iron oxide (rust) is the most usual form but there are others (black iron, purple iron yellow ochre).

Kaolin ($Al_2O_3.2SiO_2.2H_2O$)
China clay. Primary clay in its purest form.

Leather-hard
Stage during the drying process at which the clay is stiff and no longer pliable, but is still damp. In this state it can be easily handled while retaining its shape.

Majolica
Anglicization of maiolica, the decorative tin-glazed earthenware that had its roots in the medieval Islamic world but began to be widely made in Italy in the 15th and 16th centuries.

Once-fired ware
see Raw glazing.

Oxidized firing
The normal atmosphere within an electric kiln is oxidizing, meaning there is enough oxygen present to burn the fuel cleanly.

Plaster of Paris/plaster ($2CaSO_4.H_2O$)
A semi-hydrated calcium sulphate, derived from gypsum by driving off part of the water content. Used in mould making.

Plastic clay
Clay that can be manipulated but still retains its shape.

Porcelain
Highly vitrified white clay body with a high kaolin content. Developed and widely used in ancient China, its low plasticity makes it a difficult clay to work with. It can be fired as high as 1400°C (2552°F), and when thinly formed the fired body is translucent.

Pyrometer
Temperature indicator linked to a kiln via a thermocouple. Pyrometers can be analogue or digital, the latter being preferred by many potters these days.

Raw glazing
The technique of combining the biscuit firing and glaze firing in one single process. Pots treated in this way are known as once-fired ware. Glazing is usually carried out between the leather-hard and dry stages.

Reduction firing
Method of firing in a kiln fired by combustible materials such as gas, oil or wood, where the supply of oxygen is limited to prevent full combustion taking place. This produces carbon monoxide, which takes oxygen from the metals present in both clay and glaze.

Refractory
Resistant to heat, and in terms of clay, one that can be fired to high temperature without melting. Kiln bricks and shelves are made from refractory materials.

Resist
A decorative medium, such as wax, latex or paper, used to prevent slip or glaze from sticking to the surface of pottery.

Ribs
Wooden or plastic ribs are tools used to lift the walls of thrown pots, while rubber ribs are used for compacting and smoothing clay surfaces. Some ribs are kidney-shaped and may be referred to as kidneys.

Saggar
Vessel made of refractory clay used to contain pots during firing. In the ceramics industry, a "saggar maker's bottom knocker" would beat out the clay for the bases of saggars with a kind of flattened wooden mallet.

Sawdust firing
Sawdust is the fuel most often used for smoking or reducing ceramics at low temperatures.

Scrapers
Thin metal and plastic tools used to refine clay surfaces. They may be either straight or kidney-shaped, and are sometimes referred to as ribs or kidneys respectively.

Sgraffito
The cutting or scratching though an outer coating of slip, glaze or engobe to expose the different coloured body beneath. From the Italian word graffito, meaning to scratch.

Silica silicon dioxide (SiO_2)
Primary glass-forming ingredient used in glazes and also present in clay. Silica does not melt until approximately 1800°C (3272°F) and must always be used in conjunction with a flux to reduce its melting point to a workable temperature range.

Single fired
The making, glazing and firing of pottery in a single operation. Also known as raw glazing.

Slab building
Making pottery from slabs of clay.

Slip casting
Casting slip is made from clay and water, but also contains a deflocculant, allowing a reduced water content. Poured into a plaster mould, casting slip is then left to build up a shell on the inside of the mould before pouring out the excess. Remaining moisture is absorbed by the plaster.

Soaking
Time during the firing cycle when a steady temperature (often the peak) is maintained in the kiln to allow glazes to flow and mature.

Stains
Unfired colours used for decorating pottery or a ceramic pigment used to add colour to glazes and bodies.

Stilts
Small shapes of biscuit clay, sometimes with metal or wire spurs, used for supporting glazed pottery during firing.

Stoneware
Vitrified clay, usually fired above 1200ºC (2190ºF). Any glaze matures at the same time as the body, forming an integral layer.

Terracotta
An iron-bearing earthenware clay that matures at a low temperature and fires to an earth-red colour.

Terra sigillata
A very fine slip used as a surface coating for burnishing or other decorative treatments.

Throwing Clay is placed on a rotating potter's wheel and formed by hand in conjunction with centrifugal force. Throwing is said to have been developed first in Egypt c. 3000 BC

Turning/trimming
After throwing, pots are often inverted and put back on the wheel at the leather-hard stage. A metal cutting tool is used to pare off excess, cut details such as foot rings, and generally refine the form.

Underglaze
A colour usually applied to biscuit-fired pottery and in most cases covered with a glaze. A medium, such as gum arabic, is usually used to adhere the colour to biscuit but needs to be fired on prior to glazing.

Vitrification
Process by which clay materials bond to become dense, impervious and glassified during the latter part of a firing. The resulting pots are hard and durable. The vitrification point is the temperature to which a clay can be fired without deformation.

Water-based medium
Carrier that allows a pigment to be applied in the desired way. Increasingly, water-based or "water-friendly" mixtures are being used in ceramics for reasons of convenience and safety, and in preference to traditional oil-based materials, which are often rather pungent and are flammable. Various mixtures are available, often based on glycerine.

Wedging/kneading
Methods of preparing clay by hand to form a homogenous mix. It mixes clay of uneven texture and removes air pockets. Spiral kneading arranges the platelets in an advantageous way for throwing.

Index

Credits

Quarto would like to thank the following artists for kindly supplying images for inclusion in this book:

Opening spread: Jacqui Atkin
Page 2: Sue Dyer
Page 5: bottom right: Audrey Richardson;
        all others: Jacqui Atkin
Page 8: Emily Myers
Page 16: Kevin Millward
Page 31: Jacqui Atkin (pods)
Page 32: Audrey Richardson
Page 38: Peter Beard
Page 46: Charlie Atkin
Page 47: top right: Vladimir Tsivin (sculptural forms)
Page 63 bottom right: Les Rucinski (thrown vessel)
Pages 76 and 77: left-hand vessel by Jacqui Atkin;
        central vessel by Audrey Richardson;
        right-hand vessel by Jacqui Atkin
Page 84: (thrown form) Mary Chappelhow
Page 123: (thrown form) Mary Chappelhow
Page 124 (plate) Jonna Behrens
Page 126: (jug) Niek Hoogland
Page 127: Sue Dyer
Page 145: (bowls) Sasha Wardell
Page 146: (dish) Malcolm Davis

All other images are the copyright of Quarto Publishing plc. While every effort has been made to credit contributors, Quarto would like to apologize should there have been any omissions or errors – and would be pleased to make the appropriate correction for future editions of the book.

SPECIAL CREDITS
I would like to thank my daughters Nicola and Charlie for their invaluable help and support as project makers in the book and my good friend Kevin Millward for his amazing throwing expertise.
—Jacqui Atkin